PAPPY

The Days and Ways of a
Hatteras Merchant

Sybil Austin Skakle

ISBN: 978-1-962849-51-7

FOREWORD

Daddy Watcher

He did not talk much. Sometimes at the supper table he would begin to reminisce, turn his dark eyes to me and ask: "You remember him (or her) don't you?"

"No, Daddy! I do not remember!" I hated that I could not say I did.

A faded tattoo of a sailing ship on his thin chest spoke of his short stint in the U.S. Navy.

Crippled at nineteen by ankylosing spondylitis, an inflammation of the vertebra, which bent his spine into a scythe-like shape, his visions and ambitions made him dare, providing for a wife and five offspring.

With twenty-five dollars and a used Daisy barber chair, he began his 50-year business career cutting hair.

After the store closed at night, he sat in his chair, his kingdom, reading the newspaper or the books he loved.

On Sunday evenings we gathered around the radio – The Chase and Sanborn Hour, Manhattan Merry-Go-Round, and listened to Mr. Anthony. Once we read *Anne of Green Gables* as a family.

An important presence in his benevolent silence, he heard our exchanges but rarely joined our activities as Mama did -- except a jigsaw puzzle would pry him from his place and absorb his attention.

After congestive heart failure dictated more rest, he slept late while others kept his store. Many people came with questions that he, propped high on pillows, answered from his bed. Building projects caused him to rise early, eager to be on site to supervise.

He knew the ways of wood and engines; once dreamed how to repair a pesky motor, awoke and fixed it.

He built three boats: *RAMONA, SYBIL*, and *BLUE MUD,* dubbed so for its bright, azure interior. Mama wanted it named *JOMARSHA* for Josephine, Marjorie and Shanklin.

He oversaw building: the Gooseville Gun Club; the Hatteras Girl's Club, acquired a dredge to build its site; Massoletti's Cottage; Austin Theater; Durant Motor Court. During remodeling and expansion of Austin's General Merchandise Store and living quarters he did cabinet work in apartments.

Secretary-Treasurer for the inactive Woodmen of the World Lodge, members came to his store office to pay insurance year after year. Or to have him write to claim a member's death benefit.

He owned the nets (sometimes sat tying them by the chimney in the store) and boat that his elder brother and another fished.

He owned a freight boat, *Cathleen,* which carried fish to Elizabeth City, North Carolina; that transported freight back to Hatteras village. His younger brother Horton captained it for several years.

He tended Sunday dinner while we went to church and because I worried about his soul, I gave him the *St. John's Gospel* Mrs. Charlotte Ballance awarded me for learning the Beatitudes.

Once we slept at Oregon Inlet in the car overnight to catch Sunday morning's first ferry so I would not lose hope for a church school attendance pin.

Years later he told me of his conversion experience and disillusionment. The revivalist liked boys.

"Had I been able, I'd like to have been a doctor," I once heard him say. His generation had only six years of school in the village school.

"Pappy" to his grandchildren and Daddy to his own, I never doubted the love he never verbally expressed. He once painted a white doll black for his four-year-old who begged him to bring her a Black baby from Elizabeth City?

I remember his tolerance and loyalty, reliable strength and availability to his eight siblings, to his family and his friends.

Thirteen of us filled the house that 1948 summer. He piled bowls high with ice cream from the store each night as we gathered in the living room, eating all his ice cream profit and more!

We knew his expectations for us by his example: to be honest, respectable, respectful, hardworking, helpful, and kind to others.

Watching the fluid flow into his veins at Albemarle Hospital, Elizabeth City, I prayed it become the communion body and blood of Christ.

A merciful God came with others to take him HOME Sunday evening October 7, 1962.

"Sometimes he seems so close to me, I feel I can speak to him," sister Jo said one February on his birth date, as we shared our gratitude for our lightweight patriarch, who loomed large in our lives and memories.

From: *Searchings –rocks revelations rainbows- pg.* 31; Xlibris Corporation, copyright 2001.ISBN#0-7388-5863

Dedication

To my three sons: Donald Edmund, Jr., Stanley Andrew, and Clifford Dwight and their children. To my nephews, nieces, and cousins.

Kenneth Wade Oden, 1945-2004, son Josephine Austin and Carlos Desmond Oden and brother of Jeffry Lynn Oden of Hatteras first gave the name Pappy to his Austin grandfather.

Pappy belongs to many with strange names, some with no connection to Hatteras village.

Table of Contents

Chapter 1

The Village Where He Lived

My father, Andrew Shanklin Austin, loved his family and Hatteras Island, where generations of his family dreamed and thrived before him. He told Mama, Inez Lynn Daniels, born in Wanchese on Roanoke Island, "Inez, if you bury me in Wanchese, I'll swim Oregon Inlet!"

Hatteras Island is where he meant to stay. Like those who stay and endure the threats and dangers of living there, he believed it to be the most wonderful place in the world.

As a boy and youth, my father and his friends and brothers were drawn to the docks to learn from their elders, fishermen and pilots, to hang nets and to sail boats. They swam, fished, clammed, and crabbed. Their learned skills fitted them for the lives they would have, as seamen and fishermen. Every boy longed for a boat of his own.

Geologists describe Hatteras Island and the other stretches of the North Carolina Outer Banks as a sandbar. Before the New Currituck Inlet closed in 1825 and before the Hatteras and Oregon inlets were opened in 1848 by a hurricane, that sandbar stretched for two hundred miles, from the Virginia border to Ocracoke inlet, while family history unfolded.

Main Street Hatteras Village on Hatteras Island (circa 1940)

My 1948 college roommate at the University of North Carolina startled me, declaring: "Sybil, that island you came from is a foot below sea level!"

Yes, and there were times and still are when it has been/is more than a foot below sea level. During storms- north easters and hurricane - the Atlantic Ocean and Pamlico Sound merge and the lower traces of Hatteras Island disappears. The area is one of the most vulnerable places on the east coast of the United States of America.

There have been worse storms and higher tides than that 1936 September morning when our family ate breakfast with our feet ankles deep in water beneath the dining table. Two accounts, Mama's and mine, tell the story of the activity and anxiety as the tide rose to the second step of the inside stairs.

Our ancestors did not, nor do we, know how long the Indigenous people, thought to be Indians, lived on the Outer Banks before the Europeans came. Due to the darker skin tone and high cheekbones of some individuals, our family believed one of ours married or cohabitated with a native American woman.

Andrew 12 years of Age

They stole, lied, got caught, and were punished. They repented and grew wise and more compassionate. They knew the taste of soap used to wash free their mouths and tongues that lied and spoke unsavory words. They attended church on Sunday and a two-room schoolhouse, where books were scarce, but learned history and geography because they began at the beginning to study it a second time when once read.

Fed too much chicken broth as a child with scarlet fever, he had an aversion to chicken, but enjoyed the wild fowl provided by hunters for our dining table. Roast beef and Smithfield ham, oysters and old drum fish!

He had trouble saying "vinegar." His friends nick named him Vinny Gigger.

When registering for World War I draft, Daddy said he attended school for 6 years. In the 1910, when my father would have been eleven years old, his grandparents, Charles Lamb and Sallie Ann Oden, boarded a teacher, D. Coffin, a married man, from Vermont. Daddy, the schoolmaster. Was he the schoolmaster that hung boys by their thumbs for misbehaving?

During a two-week summer protracted church meeting, he became disillusioned with religion. The inappropriate attention of the revivalist to one of his friends, or to him destroyed his belief in the organized church and he did not attend church as an adult.

Tom Angel was a special part of my father's life as a young man. Tom was the only person of another race that I knew. One evening after supper, Daddy and I were alone in the kitchen, I asked him if there had ever been others and he replied: "They went away a long time ago."

In 1862, when the Civil War began, the few slaves present on Hatteras Island and surrounding areas were moved to Roanoke Island. One hundred and fifty of the men joined the Union forces.

Thomas Vine Angel, the only non-white resident of Hatteras, was never a slave. Nelson Angel came from Massachusetts, who came to keep the light burning in the lighthouse in the middle of Pamlico Sound and his wife, Inez, by an agreement with Tom's mother, brought Tom to Hatteras as their ward. Nelson Angel died in 1897.

Hatteras was home for Tom and Inez Angel was his family. He remained with her and at her death in 1912 inherited the Angel property. His remains are interred on the grounds.

Thomas Vine Angel, at his home at Hatteras

Tom Angel, a generation older than my father and his friends was a happy part of my father and his friends. They gathered at his home, a favorite gathering place. Tom entertained them, played his organ and violin and sold them ice cream he made with ice and salt and laborious turning of a crank. Cake too, I suppose.

He was elderly when he was employed to cook for members of Gooseville Gun Club. He and Luther Austin, a younger brother of my father, were true friends as they served the northern visitors.

Tom sat on the balcony of Austin Theater to watch the movies. He died in 1937 and left his cherished violin to Luther, who did not learn to play it, but loved showing it and telling stories of his friendship with Tom.

Chapter 2

Andrew's Adulthood

Andrew Shanklin Austin -- 19 years old

In the 1900s, young men and women remained with their original family until they married. Therefore, when Andrew returned to Hatteras, after a medical discharge from the United States Navy, he returned to the family home; to his parents, his six brothers, and two sisters.

His sister, Beatrice, told of their propping Andrew on pillow between two chairs to relieve his pain. They did not know what caused his suffering. His family thought his pain due to his having stayed wet all the way to South America and back. The card from his registration for the World War I draft in 1914 reads: "deformity due to rheumatism." Ankylosing spondylitis is a type of arthritis of the spine that causes inflammation and gradual fusing of the vertebrae.

His Business Beginning

In 1908, my father invested twenty-five-dollars in a second-hand barber chair, purchased in "Little Washington," North Carolina. Eugene Beringhaus of Cincinnati, Ohio, a company that sold barber furniture between 1902-1912, had built the chair. Red velvet covered the seat and back or the chair and a metal plate attached to the wooden frame beneath the seat identified it as *Daisy*. Daisy remained part of the store furnishings of the story for all the store years. Daddy recovered it with a blue denim first. At the end he used a black leather-like to cover the seat and back.

The U.S. Navy may have trained him to cut hair. He may have learned on his own, as a boy at home, cutting his brothers' hair. Surely, he had some reason to buy a barber chair.

His uncle, Singleton Oden, sold him the building that would serve as his barber shop. It had to be moved from the Oden yard to a place opposite Bascom Ballance's store and Gaskin's graveyard. To move the building with horse and poles through the sand must have been an impressive undertaking. It might be compared to the relocation of the Cape Hatteras Lighthouse by a crew of savvy engineers in 1998 to safer site, to save it from the encroachment of the Atlantic Ocean.

The sand in front of that graveyard was the deepest and softest in the village. As a small girl, I nearly fell face first in a rut as I tried to get past faster. I feared the dead. "It isn't the dead, but the wagging tongues of the living one needs to fear!" Mama said.

Hatteras village did not have a bank until 1970. Due to efforts of Albert (Bert) Austin, East Carolina erected a bank on the former Singleton Oden property next door to the A. S. Austin Store. Plantar Bank in Buxton had been in business only a few years.

In the 1900s my father invested his money in a bit of tangible merchandise to be sold from his barber shop: candy, socks, and the detachable white shirt collars that young men of that era wore. Without having studied economics, he discerned the practicality of supplying a demand. His confectionary venture must have waited for his move to larger quarters.

Evidence of such a venture existed in 1930. There were bottles of chocolate, strawberry, vanilla, orange, and root beer syrups and a couple of twisted wire chairs with round bottoms familiar to soda fountains.

Once when I was a small girl, Daddy made a milkshake without ice cream for me. He shaved ice with a handheld metal ice shaver from a clump. This he dumped into a Mason jar, added canned evaporated milk and chocolate syrup. With vigorous shaking the mixture produced a tasty milkshake.

Chapter 3

A New Decade and His Interest in Land

In 1910, Georgia A. Gaskins, the wife of W. H. Gaskins, sought a grant of an extensive tract of Hatteras land. My father lodged a protest. It is believed he did so because some of the property she requested had been granted to early ancestors of his family.

Thomas Austin received grants in 1755 and 1756; William Benjamin Ballance, Jr., who migrated from Currituck to Hatteras Banks earlier than Austin, was said to have acquired land that extended "from Cape Hatteras all the way to Ocracoke Inlet," and he purchased a large tract from Susannah Stowe in 1785.

William Springer Stowe (1770-1855), father of my father's great-grandmother, Lovie Stowe, owned property on the south side of Austin Creek that extended to Hatteras Inlet.

My father's successful defense against the Georgia A. Gaskins grant claim of 1910 began his lifelong interest in land history and acquisition.

In 1912, Daddy went to Hot Springs, Arkansas, for treatment.

In the picture, made at the Army-Navy Hospital, my father is seated far right on the edge of the bed. His spine is not as curved as it would become.

Chapter 4

Inez Lynn Daniels

Inez Lynn Daniels, student, 1910-1911

While my father, Andrew, was meeting his challenges, Inez Lynn Daniels, whom he would meet in the early or late summer of 1912, either before or after he had spent time at Hot Spring, Arkansas for treatment, had attended school at North Carolina Normal School in Greensboro, North Carolina

Something called phrenology helped Inez Lynn achieve her dream of more education. Phrenology, practiced during the late 1800s and into the next century, is the study of the contours of the skull.

One day a phrenologist came by the Wanchese homestead of George Charles and Margaret Johnson Daniels. After studying the skull of their daughter Inez, the phrenologist told them that the contour and irregularities of her skull indicated notable intelligence. Inez and her family began to explore ways and means to obtain additional education for Inez.

Dr. Franklin Pierce Gates (1859- 1922), a Manteo physician engaged to her elder sister Elrado, gave or loaned Inez twenty dollars to get her to school. With two blouses and a skirt, she left Wanchese by boat to Elizabeth City and by train to Greensboro, to attend North Carolina Normal School, the school Charles McIver championed for the education of women. She worked in the school dining room to earn her tuition, room, and board and during the 1910-1911 school year her horizons broadened and her "wings" grew strong.

Inez returned to Dare County, took a county exam and received her teacher's certificate. Her first teaching assignment was in Edward, North Carolina.

Her niece, Sallie Montague, daughter of her half-sister, Lucetta Daniels Tillett, had been invited to visit two young women, Lovie and Beatrice Austin of Hatteras. She invited Inez to go with her and told her about their unmarried, exceptionally good-looking older brother.

Inez was interested. She visited her friend Annie Springer, at Springer's Point in Ocracoke one summer and had been interested in

Annie's brother. It seemed a mutual attraction but had been only a summer flirtation for both.

When Inez met the Austin family she had been startled by Andrew's appearance. The man Sallie described so glowingly seemed stooped by age. After hearing his story, she decided he may have injured his spine as a youth working at Wainwright's porpoise factory. While lying flat on his stomach, he grabbed a porpoise by the tail from a fisher on a boat and flipped it onto the dock behind him. Pain and inflammation of the spine accounted for his disfigurement.

During Inez's visit, her compassion became affection and Andrew, fishing in waters near Wanchese, visited her home. He and her father became so engrossed in conversation that she asked him: "Whom did you come to see? Poppa or me?"

In either 1912 or 1913, Inez accepted a teaching position in lower Dare County in the wooded village of Trent. With the establishment of the post office in 1898, the village had been renamed Frisco, but the village residents still call themselves "Trenters."

She arrived by mail boat and was welcomed by Minerva and William Leonard Whedbee into their home. The Whedbee home and the one-room school, on the Pamlico Sound side of the village, were an easy walk for her and Trent was accessible to Andrew with his horse, Deck, and his wagon. (I once climbed on the discarded wagon in our back yard.) Sand ruts and mosquitoes made the four miles to Trent seem more like twenty, in any kind of weather.

One moon shining night as Andrew was returning home from Trent with Deck and the wagon. He approached the "back road," as it was called, and the hill where dipping vat, used to rid livestock of vermin, was located, he had a scare. A woman with long, flowing hair stood there beckoning him. Andrew urged Deck forward, insistently.

The next day he went back to look. He discovered a straggly tree which had been made eerie by the moonlight.

My mother may have taught only one year at Frisco; maybe two. My father's timeline gives December 9, 1914, as the date of their marriage. Neither Wanchese nor Hatteras could be reached except by boat. Their trip may have required two stages for them to reach Elizabeth City, where they were married.

Chapter 5

Life of Young Marrieds

After their marriage, Andrew took Inez home to his parents' household up the road. The household already held three unmarried brothers: Nacie, Luther, and Horton and married siblings Beatrice (Leo) and Monroe (Katherine), and at least one baby.

Their son, Andrew Shanklin, Jr., was born December 26, 1915. Monroe's first child, Mogieannah, and Beatrice's first child, Leo Wallace Peele, Jr., arrived while they were still part of the intergenerational family.

Babies Mogieannah and Shanklin Baby Shanklin

The Bascom Ballance family home sat south of the Wheeler Austin home, and the home of Willie Gaskins and his wife, Georgia Anna Midgette, sat across the road from the Ballance home. They may have been the only homes in that area of the road at the time.

Hatteras village had two churches, the Southern Methodist Church, in the center of the village, and the Northern Methodist Episcopal Church, located in the southern part of the village. Inez attended the one closest to the Austin home, the Southern Methodist; her father-in-law expressed dismay: "If you keep attending that church, you'll soon be wearing silk dresses bought with another man's money!"

"Why Mr. Wheeler, I wouldn't mind having a silk dress!" Inez replied, with a twinkle in her eye.

My father's grandfather, William Dudley Austin, Jr., served in the Union Army during the Civil War. The Austins' loyalty was to the Northern Methodist Episcopal church, where Mogieannah's younger brother, Dexter Oden, and his wife Alice served as faithful custodians for as long as they lived. My mother's family had been sympathetic to the Confederacy.

Called "the down-below church," the Northern Methodist Episcopal church washed off its foundation in the 1933 or the 1936 hurricane. We sometimes went to the afternoon church school there. Ministers of both churches were guests at our dinner table. Regularly, we attended the church across the road and next to the schoolhouse. In 1939 the two churches became The Methodist Church.

The Holy Bible was the only book the Austin family owned, but Inez brought a trunkful of books with her from Wanchese. She and Andrew read together in their bedroom.

It is supposed the family kept chickens. There was a horse and cart, certainly. However, they did not keep hogs. Mama's farmer father sometimes sent Inez a ham. They may have maintained a small vegetable garden. Collards grow well, even in the sandy soil. By my time of memory and when I was a small girl cows and horses roamed free. The livestock that was not kept up was evicted from the island sometime after 1930. The Austin family had fish, beans, and chicken enough, but it would be a long while before the island stores had regular supplies of fresh meats. They had no refrigeration to care for fresh meat, but cured hams were part of their food supply.

Chapter 6

A New Business and New Living Quarters

*This was drawn from 1923 taken by the photographer accompanying
General Billy Mitchell*

In 1916 Andrew bought a lot, situated across the road from the schoolhouse where Inez taught. His uncle Singleton Oden sold him property of "one acre, more or less" east of his own lot and next to the Methodist Church parsonage.

Andrew drew plans and Inez loaned him five hundred dollars to build. Her half-brother, Ethelbert (Tucker) Daniels of Wanchese, would build their dwelling, as well as a home for Andrew's brother Monroe, next to their father and mother's home. Daniels would build, across the road from Monroe's home, a third two-storied building for the Woodmen of the World, an active organization at Hatteras then and is viable insurance company. All three buildings were painted white with maroon shingled trim.

In early 1918, Inez and Andrew, with their young son Shanklin, moved into their unfinished, new quarters. The pandemic Spanish flu, during which the Eco-Health Organization reported five hundred million people worldwide fell sick and between three and five percent of the world's population died, was raging. That pandemic lasted for fifteen months. They were expecting a second child and Marjorie Hope arrived March 28, 1918.

The Store Layout

In Daddy's elevated office at the back of the store, a large window overlooked the back yard, where a two-car, unpainted garage faced toward the ocean. Later, a single car garage, painted white, would face the driveway from the road.

Across from Daddy's desk and chair a large black safe sat in the right-hand corner. In front of the window, facing the front of the store, a half-partition, with glass in the upper part, enabled Daddy, sitting at his desk, to see both sides at the front of the store; looking over top of the cash and charge registers, which sat onto the main floor. The registers faced toward the office. The shelves on the outer office wall held patented medicines and school supplies.

In the main part of the store, on the left side beyond the registers, was a ladder that ran on metal tracks in the ceiling behind counters. The wall shelves held dry goods, bolts of cloth, notions and shoes. At Christmas time those shelves held exciting things for little girls to see and touch.

Shelves on the same wall as Daddy's safe, but on the main floor, behind the registers, held food stuffs, canned goods and packaged ones. On the floor, beneath those shelves were bins that held three kinds of dried beans: lima, navy and black-eyed peas.

On a corner of the counter in front of those shelves and nearest the registers a set of scales sat. The scales had a heavy glass counter and a set of weights to counterbalance things to be weighed. The candy showcase sat on the other corner at the front of the store, near an empty room.

The shed door was behind the registers and on the same wall as the shelves. In the shed, opposite the door, were two 50-gallon barrels, against the wall. The wooden barrel, with a wooden pump, held vinegar. The other was a metal and held molasses, which fermented one summer and ran out onto the shed floor. Left of the barrels and next to the only window, stood a wooden chopping block, which held a slab of salt pork and a sharp knife.

On the corner of a counter, just inside the shed door, stood round wooden box, which held a round of cheddar cheese. On the same counter were fifty-pound bags of sugar and flour. Sugar and four had to be measured into paper bags and weighed, as did the chicken feed, which lay on the right side of the shed on the floor and poured into metal bound, measuring containers: quart, peck, gallon. The shed door stood beyond.

Another door gave access to the back porch as well. From behind the wall against which Daddy's office desk sat, a door gave access to a 50-gallon metal barrel of kerosene; to be pumped into his customers' five-gallon containers for their cook stoves. Each Saturday their kerosene and the rest of their weekly grocery order was delivered, first by horse and cart and then by car. Few people owned cars. (Ellsworth Burrus owned the first car and Daddy owned the second one at Hatteras.)

Thrift and industry enabled Daddy to acquire a remarkable variety in his small inventory. Not only did he sell groceries, dry goods, patent medicines but he added kegs of nails, gum boots, paint, boat engine fittings, glass to be cut to size, which were stored in the very back of the store to the right of the back door. A cobbler's iron shoe form sat on a counter above the nail kegs. Did Daddy repair shoes for customers?

A stalk of bananas hung from the ceiling and a basket of fresh cabbage sat on the in front of the counter with the scales. Seasons of harvest limited fresh fruit availability a hundred years ago. An orange in the toe of a Christmas stocking was a special treat. But I remember bananas!

Another Decade and Another Baby

Josephine, a second daughter, arrived January 25, 1921. Leah Ballance, a local midwife, delivered this baby. Daddy asked that she be named after a nurse he had in Arkansas, named Josephine Leggett. Mama objected to the second name. "We have a shank. We will not have a Leggett!" she declared.

Christening day came and Daddy persisted, but Mama won. Josephine was the baby's only given name at christening.

A week after Josephine's birth, February 1, 1921, a five-masted commercial schooner, *Carroll A. Deering,* hauling coal ran aground off Cape Hatteras. The Gulf Stream, favored by ships for faster eastward travel, runs closer to Hatteras Island than it does to other bodies of land on the East Coast. Diamond Shoals, abreast of Hatteras is called the Graveyard of the Atlantic. The shoals are a threat to water transportation. Storms and strong currents cause vessels of every size to run aground. The sand quickly grasps them fast.

When crew members from Cape Hatteras Coast Guard Station boarded the vessel, only a cat roaming the deck. The *Deering* became known as "the ghost ship" by locals and romantic journalists and the mystery surrounding the ship's crew remains unsolved.

A group of local men planned to go aboard the *Deering* after the regular salvagers had completed their work. Daddy very much wanted to be part of that adventure. Mama agreed to tend store despite having her hands full with a new baby, plus Shank, an active little boy of six, and Margie, four years old.

While Mama waited for Daddy to return, she entertained visions of a sturdy set of flatware to set her dinner table. Alas, when Daddy came home late that afternoon, his pockets were full of matches. He bore no treasure for Mama. "I kept hoping to find something better!" he explained, apologetically.

Daddy would buy treasures from the salvagers. Several items from the *Deering* besides Daddy's large, handsome oak desk and chair, were part of the furnishings of the upstairs over the store. A clawfoot bathtub was placed inside a small bedroom at the back west side of the house. Two ship washstands were used in bedrooms instead of washstands with bowls and pitchers.

Four oak drawers were fitted into a wooden frame at the top of the stairs above the store area. A glass-doored bookcase that held a well-worn *Mother Goose* and other books sat on top of the counter that held the drawers, used to store linens for the house.

(During renovation and expansion of the building in the early 1940s, the four oak drawers were fitted into a more compact frame, with a two-door bookcase.)

Water for the bathroom had to be hand pumped into the wooden tank Daddy had installed in the attic above the bathroom. One day, probably a Saturday, Daddy hired some boys to do the pumping. Brother Shank may have helped.

Daddy had a tan stone crock where his home brew was fermenting in the attic. The boys decided to sample Daddy's home brew. Mama must have been alerted by the smell of alcohol on the person of her son. She doused Daddy's home brew with kerosene and waited in trepidation.

Frustrated and agitated, his face flushed, his dark eyes flashing, Daddy confronted Mama, "Inez, you've done it this time!" he said, shaking his head.

"Yes, and I'll do it again," she replied. "I am not going to raise our children around that stuff!"

Eventually, the stone crock, filled with sand, sat by the two homemade benches in the middle of the store. I never knew it to hold anything other than sand and burned cigarette butts.

Mama's father, George Charles Daniels, shared his wisdom, garnered from watching his farm animals. "Daughter, I have observed that the hog that makes the least noise at the feeding trough gets the most food."

He knew his strong-willed daughter managed to get things her way. Once, as a small girl, she climbed a pear tree and ate the pear he hoped to grow lush and ripe. She left the stem. When confronted, she truthfully replied. "I didn't pick it, Dad!"

Mama, who continued to teach school and earn money, reminded Daddy that he had never repaid the five hundred dollars she loaned him to build the house. Daddy chuckled. "Inez, you've been repaid over and over again!" he replied.

My mother still longed to have that money in the palm of her right hand. As far as I know, that never happened.

While Mama taught, she had help at home. She would have help in future years when she kept the house full of roomers and boarders. Her story tells best of the condition of the two-room schoolhouse across the road. From *Then and Now*

Chapter 7

"The School Across the Road"
Author: Inez Daniels Austin

Parsonage, Methodist Church and Hatteras School (1923)

The things of yesteryear we consider Then. The things of the present we think of as Now. Just now I am considering my surroundings of two eras. Across the road stood a two-room schoolhouse, a stranger to paint, a stranger to grades.

Two teachers taught seven grades. One teacher had from the six-year group through the ten-year group. Now we call those groups grades. One through the fourth. The other teacher had the rest of the children, eleven to sixteen years.

One never got as far as high school. But those fourteen-, fifteen-, and sixteen-year-old (children) knew their books. They should! Sometimes they did one book over again as much as three times.

Pretty much the same was true with the first four years of work. Repeat and repeat was the order of the educational system. I thought I would never leave the big geography and big history behind or any of the other subjects for that matter.

Folks know a lot more about sanitation now than then. The toilet facilities were zero. No one had to wash their hands after restroom visits. The only water available was a wooden water bucket, bought at the beginning of school. A tin dipper was the common property of all. All drank and dipped in the cooling draught, never a thought of a germ. In fact, I cannot recall that the word germ was given much credence then.

Each of the outhouses, one for girls and one for boys, had two or three holes over open ground. This was before outdoor toilets were placed over deep dug enclosed pits.

The neighbor's hogs usually did a cleanup job each night. Sometimes they went inside, smearing up the place. Sometimes the outhouse was overturned. I do not believe the hogs did that though. I imagine the neighborhood boys thought the hogs were having more fun than they were. Or perhaps they hoped not to go to school for a day or two. This was not always the case, however. The hiding places for children then were to be for a few days under the schoolhouse, behind the bushes or rushes or out behind the church.

It was a real treat that high tides swept over the land occasionally. The salt in the tide must have been a good way to do away with some of the vermin that the hogs did not devour. The sun, too, would be a good means of purifying salt air. This area has ample sunshine and salty air. No one has died of any communicable disease, or otherwise, caused by unhealthy sanitation conditions.

We may be just lucky people to be here on the edge of what many people might term "nowhere." Not so to the people here, to be sure. They think there is no place this side of heaven as dear to the hearts of humans.

The quiet, the peace and isolation of yesteryear is constantly changing with the coming of a road through the villages. And soon a bridge to ride over the long-time ferry service inlet. All things change yearly.

Not many years ago, we had no such help as mosquito control. Anyone who sat out at night sat by a smoke and killed mosquitoes, with that preventive failing to take care of the whole problem satisfactorily. Now the sprayer (truck with a sprayer) goes through the village puffing out deadly fumes to the fly and mosquito nuisance.

We used to have an iron smoke pot out on the front of side yard. The smoke was made up of old woolen socks, pants, old shoes, cow dung or anything that made a strong smell. Perhaps each household should have had two or three pet skunks to save a lot of labor and kill off the pests of the evening, also.

Chapter 8

Two More Daughters- Mama's Second Family

Five-year-old Jo started school early and Mama continued to teach until expecting a fourth child. Hatteras Island had no doctor. She and other expectant mothers relied on a young United States Navy pharmacist mate, Maurice Bernard Folb, authorized to administer first aid. Ably, he delivered babies in the villages and returned to the United States Naval Radio Station in Buxton, ten miles north of Hatteras, to write up his first aid reports.

Maurice Bernard Folb delivered a ten-pound baby girl at 2:45 a/m on January 10, 1926, in one of the seven upstairs bedrooms of the two-story maroon-and-white dwelling in the middle of Hatteras Village. I was named Sybil Bernadine for the him and his wife, Sybil Miller of Buxton.

(Charlie Wood Austin at far left and Luther Austin, seated in chair, left of the two conversing.)

Queen Elizabeth was also born in 1926 and a 40-hour work week began. Calvin Coolidge was president of the United States. Hirohito was crowned emperor of Japan; Robert Goddard launched the first successful liquid fuel rocket; and A. A. Milne first published "Winnie-the-Pooh."

Sybil with Maurice Bernard Folb at Austin Reunion Picnic circa 1982-1984

In 1927, before I had been weaned, Mama needed to leave me to have gall bladder surgery in Norfolk, Virginia. I was left in the care of Daddy's older brother, Monroe, and his wife Katie.

At that time, Mama's surgeon removed several gall stones, but not the gall bladder. Daddy kept the stones in a small drawer of his desk, and I climbed into his office chair and onto his desk to look at them when no one was around.

In early 1929, Mama had another gall bladder attack that sent her back to the hospital in Norfolk, Virginia. She was not expected to live after the removal of her gall bladder. Daddy decided he needed to take their children for their final goodbye. He alerted Toby Tillett of Wanchese, who had begun ferry service across Oregon Inlet.

Toby Tillett's ferry for crossing from Hatteras Island to the mainland.

The ferry docked on the north side of Oregon Inlet. When a motorist arrived at the landing area, they raised the flag positioned there to alert Toby to come across Oregon Inlet to take them back across. Toby's residence was in Wanchese. Daddy must have contacted him somehow of his need to get across before he left Hatteras, because it was still dark as we passed Kill Devil Hill. I was drowsing on sister Marjorie's lap in the back seat of the car with Josephine. Shank was up front with Daddy.

Mama told the story of her discomfort when Daddy brought us. Having discovered elevators, we were keeping the elevator attendant busy riding us up and down in the wonderful box. Mama fretted, unable to do anything about it.

Mama did not die. During her discharge, her surgeon said, "Mrs. Austin, you will probably lose your baby. Mama did not know she was expecting a baby. She replied, "I bet I don't!"

Daddy had been told Mama's life expectancy without a gall bladder was at most two years. Ramona had been born several years before Mama knew of that dire prediction.

Daddy's heart condition had worsened and he fretted about it. One night Mama felt his tears wetting her face, after then had retired. She asked why he was crying.

"I am thinking about what is to become of our children." Daddy's heart condition had worsened and he supposed his days were numbered.

Mama could not have him crying. So many years as a schoolteacher and parent, she attempted to reassure him. "Well, I will take care of our children, Andrew. Now you stop crying."

"But the doctor said you would die without your gall bladder."

The Birth of the Baby, a Fourth Daughter, and the Hatteras doctor

Dr. H. W. Kenfield and his wife Blanche Badgley had arrived from Michigan to be our doctor before 1929. I was still the baby in the family the day I remember so vividly. Dr. Kenfield was walking by the fence and he called to me, playing in the front yard, "Come over here, Sybil, let me see your eye."

Trustingly, I went to the fence, stood on the bottom piece for him to look into my eye at the angry stye. He reached over and holding my head steady with one hand, popped the stye in my right eye with fingers of his nicotine-stained other hand. I screamed. I was one angry little girl. Surely, he did not do what he did without having been prompted by Mama.

He would be the one who attended Mama when the baby was due and Mama's older sister, Elrado, came to help Mama. It was not the birth of Cecelia Ramona being born that I remembered about November 12, 1929, when I was almost four. Being able to sleep with Aunt Rado in the bedroom off the upstairs living room without removing my clothes was the event I celebrated that evening.

Over the following years we relied on him for our emergencies and for spring doses of calomel, to clean our systems. He removed a large splinter from Mona's leg and he stitched up Josephines foot, sliced open by a broken glass jar on the bottom of Rollinson Creek.

We had been swimming. I was watching where Jo jumped from the side of the boat into the water when the broken jar lay.

Dr. Kenfield had a lovely new house built on the west bank of Slash Creek, with a separate office building that matched the design of the house, after the one in which he first lived burned to the ground. They moved into their new quarters in 1932.

A 1937 newspaper clipping reported that Dave Driscoll, an employee of Albert Lyons of Gooseville Gun Club, had flown Dr. H. W. Kenfield to Elizabeth City because of illness. The article also noted: "Andrew S. Austin took three youths from Hatteras to Elizabeth City to give blood to save Dr. Kenfield's life."

Dr Kenfield died of pneumonia August 22, 1937. He was 60 years of age. His grave is in Elmwood Cemetery in Charlotte, North Carolina.

People talked about his Camel cigarette smoking and his foibles but depended on his service. Dr. H. W. Kenfield also served as village magistrate, the only representative of the law the village had.

Chapter 9

Elrado Daniels

Elrado Daniels, born February 19, 1879, was my mother's older sister and part of my life, always. She is important. My mother relied on her and she was always part of my prayers, taught by Mama: "This night I lay me down to sleep. I pray, Thee Lord, my soul to keep. If I should die before I wake, I pray, Thee Lord, my soul to take. Bless Mama and Daddy, brother and sister, Jo and Aunt Rado. Make Sybil and Mona good little girls. In Jesus name I pray. Amen."

Elrado's father, Ezekiel Rollins Daniels, and her mother were never married. Margaret gave birth to Elrado five months after Zeke married Elizabeth Ann Pugh, June 15, 1880. Both were related to George. And when he and Margaret married, George claimed her as his daughter. They were blood kin.

Elrado may have avoided the hateful remarks children make by not attending school. She never learned to read and write. It was supposed that having been dropped on her head when a baby prevented her from learning. As an adult, she kept strict account of her money and managed her dressmaking and boarding house businesses well.

Visiting her one summer, as I loved to do, I took shoes to be repaired. I paid the cobbler when I gave him my shoes. I returned to her and she questioned me and said, "Never pay for the work until the work is done!"

Elrado, a handsome woman, told me she loved to dance and once loaned her shoe to a boy so they could go dancing. When I asked why she never married, she answered: "Had I married I would have been expected to have children. Children ache your arms as babies and your heart when they are older."

But another time, she smiled and added: "I could not marry them all."

She had been engaged to Dr. Franklin Pierce Gates (1859-1922), a widower twenty years older than she. Once, after he returned from a trip away from Roanoke Island, he questioned her loyalty. She believed she caused his death at sixty-three, because, in her anger at him, she had put a curse on him. Years later, she gave Myrtle, her niece, Lillian's daughter, the engagement ring Gates had given her.

A loving, generous woman, Elrado did not like to have anyone leave her home empty handed. Once she gave Mama a box of round Hi Ho crackers. Aunt Rado's round tan ones tasted better than the square Nabisco "soda crackers" from Daddy store.

Elrado Daniels and her fiancé, Dr. Franklin Pierce Gates, circa 1910

While Mama and Daddy traveled to California, in the summer of 1936, I stayed with her in a large, square white house on the corner of Main Street in Berkley, Virginia. The porch wrapped around the front and right side of the house. In the yard, to the right of the side porch, stood and enormous China Berry Tree, which I climbed and picked berries. Aunt Rado showed me how to boil them and extract the inside kernel. I strung them and they made a handsome necklace. She taught me to crochet that summer.

Her roomers were Guy Ireland, a chief in the U. S. Coast Guard; a young married couple expecting their first child; and an older man, Mr. Bottome, a widower.

Mr. Bottome died while still living with her. He may have pawned his dead wife's jewelry, or Aunt Rado may have needed to pawn it to pay for his burial. She urged Mama to buy it out of pawn.

Mama bought a ring with sixteen diamonds and an amethyst brooch. She planned to have rings made for her four daughters by dividing the cluster. However, Josephine, sixteen years old, put the ring on her finger and wore it for the rest of her the rest of her 97 years and Marjorie was given the amethyst brooch. When Mama died, Ramona claimed her golden wedding band. Mama never treasured clothes or jewelry for herself.

Guy, a boarder that summer, seemed like another uncle to me, because he remained part of Aunt Rado's life. He always called her "Miss Daniels. However, he had moved from her boarding house when his divorced sister, Leola, returned to Norfolk and went to live with her. He came to visit Aunt Rado in the evening.

She lived on a different street in another two-story house when I visited her as World War II began. Still in Berkley, her roomers were men working in the Norfolk shipyard. Guy came to visit in the evening.

Aunt Rado returned to Wanchese in her final years. I visited her in nursing-home and then at Aunt Lillian's.

Aunt Lillian's store and living quarters, located on Wanchese's main thoroughfare, included two bedrooms. Her sewing machine sat in the "store-living room" area. I visited them there. Then, Myrtle Tillett decided she, not her elderly mother, should care for Aunt Rado.

When I last saw Aunt Rado at Myrtle's she wore a pink bow in her hair and smelled of Wind Song. She was joyful! She died in April before reaching her one hundredth birthday the following February.

Chapter 10

Family Life and Raising Children

Mama usually made decisions concerning us children. Once, however, she sent me to have Daddy decided if I was to spend the night with my cousin and playmate Anna Ballance.

"Go ask your father. If he says it is all right, you may go."

Juanita, Anna's mother, and Mama's niece had stayed and helped when the first three children were young, for Mama to teach.

Josephine, Mama, Juanita Tillett and Marjorie standing and Shank, seated by the oak tree by the front fence. Circa 1923.

She is with them in another picture taken at Durant Coast Guard Station, by the photographer with General Billy Mitchell in 1923, when he came with pilots and airplanes to prove a ship can be sunk by an airplane.

Anna's family lived with her fraternal grandfather, Jardella Balance. He owned a store up the road. His store, not large or thriving, did not threaten Daddy's business, but it had something that Daddy 's store did not have. Neat, the name I called Juanita because Mama did, brought Anna and me black walnut candy from his store, as we sat on the linoleum floor, cutting paper dolls from an old Sear Roebuck catalogue one day.

I loved visiting Anna. Neat's breakfasts of hot biscuits and oatmeal, and her hambone soup, delighted my palate. Other people, their lives, and their food fascinated me.

So, if I were to go, I had to ask Daddy, sitting at his desk, in the elevated office at the back of the store. "Daddy, Mama said I could spend the night with Anna if it is all right with you."

No. I don't want you to go," he said. might try to wheedle Mama, but not Daddy. I turned away, disappointed, crying, as I went back to be comforted by Mama.

Mama claimed she spoiled all five of us. True, she did, because she avowed: "It is easier to please a fool than to plague one."

Mama's spoiling did not interfere with her training us to be orderly and cooperative. We were assigned jobs appropriate to our abilities and were treated respectfully and kindly. She would inquire: "Would you like to do this for me?"

How could I possibly say, "NO!" when asked so politely by my loving mother.

Mama rarely baked and Daddy loved sweets. Once, he decided to stir up a raisin cake. He kept adding ingredients until the consistency of his batter looked right and ended up with enough cake to feed his original family, eleven individuals. We enjoyed his cake. None was wasted.

That Daddy did not go to church troubled me. He stayed home and watched the roast. I feared he might not make Heaven. Mrs. Charlotte Ballance awarded me a little red booklet of *The Gospel of St. John* for memorizing The Beatitudes. I took it home and gave it to Daddy. (We did not have worship every Sunday. We shared our minister with two other churches of the charge.)

A grown woman, I asked Daddy why he never attended church. The improper conduct of a visiting, summer revivalist toward one of his friends or himself resulted in his disillusionment. He lost faith in religion.

Mama and Daddy, trained by the adage, "Waste not that you want not," did not waste God-given resources. They were careful and frugal. Mama turned every cloth sack that came to the store with flour, sugar, or meal into something useful: pillowcases, sheets, underwear. Pajamas?

She pieced quilt tops from scraps from her sewing and discarded clothing on her New Home sewing machine. One Christmas she dressed every doll Mona and I had. The pink chiffon dress she made for my long-legged hard-body doll had tiny pearl buttons at the neckline.

Conservation prevailed. Mama picked up boards and other treasures. She stored the boards above the rafters in the wash house and probably found a use for every piece before the proverbial seventh year.

Inez Lynn Daniels Austin – Mama (circa 1936)

Salary vs. Allowance

Daddy said, "We share alike. We all contribute to the family, and we all benefit."

Daddy did not think Mama should pay Mona and me a dollar a week to help. Mama, however, with her schoolteacher training and delight in earning wages, had another view. She believed that the dollar as a wage, not an allowance, would help us appreciate working. Daddy, an astute businessman, surrendered to Mama's argument.

Feeling very grown up, I made out my first order from the Montgomery Ward catalogue for identical dresses for Mona and me. The dresses had navy blue skirts with attached printed blouses trimmed in navy blue cloth like our skirts. We were proud to have bought our own clothes. When Christmas time came, we went Christmas shopping at Mr. Dan Oden's store.

One day I did not want to remember my employee responsibility. I wanted to quit! My friends came by to swim in the ocean and invited me to go. I wanted to go, even though I had gone with Ms. Maude O'Neal, the Hatteras "postmaster," early that morning to swim in the Pamlico Sound. Mama had other plans for me that day. (Ms. Maude insisted on "postmaster." She declared, "I have never been mistress to any man!")

Mama was wallpapering the downstairs living room. She had already covered the ridges of the wooden walls with newspaper, glued in place with homemade flour paste. She was ready to paste on the commercial product and insisted I stay to help her. Of course, I did!

Mama could be firm. She did not let me have my way when I wanted to stay at school at lunch time. A little boy I fancied brought his lunch to school. His family's home was too distant for him and his siblings to go home. One day I stayed at school. The second day, Mama confronted me. She expected me to come home for lunch, and thereafter I did.

Sharing the Load

Monday was washing day unless it rained. Everyone's dirty clothing, sheets, pillowcases, covers, and towels were collected and carried to the wash house to be sorted into piles. Whites were washed first and the lightest and cleanest next. Heavy work clothing found the suds last.

Navy beans were always washday fare. Covered in water with salt pork for seasoning, the beans were cooked slowly over a low flame while the washing progressed.

A large, galvanized wash tub, propped on bricks over an open fire stood next to the walkway that ran from the kitchen door to the washhouse door. A sturdy wooden stick, perhaps a former mop handle, was used to stir the clothing and remove the hot masses from the tub to be transported to the first tub of cold water inside the washhouse. A washboard and a bar of lye soap were there for clothing that needed more scrubbing. Wringing clothes by hand required every muscle of arm and hand.

The second tub of cold water contained bluing, to make the whites seem whiter. A final rinse removed excess bluing and clothing was ready for the cotton lines, strung across the yard from branches of trees to catch the breezes and sunlight. Clothespins attached washed items to the lines, overlapping one piece under another to save clothespins and space.

Articles that needed starching were held back. Dresses, shirt collars, table covers, and pillowcases! Argo starch and cold water had been mixed and boiling water added to produce a smooth gelatinous solution of the right density and proper volume for the clothing needing it.

Clotheslines strung between the rafters in the attic received clothing that did not dry sufficiently outdoors. Sometimes unexpected rain or evening damp made further drying necessary.

Dry starched clothing was sprinkled with cold water and wrapped in a bundle for ironing the following day.

Mama enjoyed many things more than she did cooking, and Daddy teased: "You hire Dell Rollison to do the wash, then let Dell cook dinner, while you wash the clothes."

Dry beans needed little tending. Mama and Ms. Dell may have taken turns stirring the beans while they enjoyed washing clothes and visiting. Washing, done well, is a beautiful process and produces sweet-smelling, clean clothing reward.

When people complain about doing laundry, or cleaning the house, I smile in wonder. Machines have delivered us from the hard labor of the past.

House Cleaning

Every spring the house hummed with activity. Mattresses were aired outside on the porches. Blankets and spreads were hung outside in the sunshine all day to freshen them after winter's use. The springs on the bed were swept free of dirt. Furniture was rearranged. Mama loved d change and Daddy claimed he had to be extra careful during spring cleaning lest he end up on the floor trying to go to bed. The whole house was torn apart before it was put back together again. Good housekeepers followed this pattern of activity every spring.

Our Water Supply

Our water supply depended on the rainwater that ran off the roof into the gutters and through the downspout into the cistern. An alcove, off the room that served as both kitchen and dining area, held a hand driven pump that brought water from the cistern outside the kitchen-dining room window on the east side of the house.

The cistern, built of cement, sat mostly above ground. When water was low in the cistern, we poured water into the top of the pump to prime it. When the water level was extremely low, wigglers (mosquitoes' larvae) came out of the spout, and we knew the cistern must be cleaned to be ready for rain.

Chapter 11

Drummers and Boarders- Mama's New Activity

Sybil Holding a Dead Waterfowl

Daddy and Mama must have had plans, other than Mama's childhood notion that she wanted nine sons, when they had the two-story dwelling and store built in the middle of the village. The building had eight bedrooms and a living room upstairs above the store area.

Visitors to the island were cared for in private homes and E. Ellsworth Burrus had not yet built the Atlantic View Hotel. It would not be built until 1928.

Sales associates, men called "drummers," and now known as detailers, needed overnight lodgings. Sportsmen, hunters and fishermen, from other parts of the United States had discovered the rewards of hunting and fishing on the remote island of Hatteras. Several hunting clubs were built up and down the Dare County coast during this era.

During 1900s, parlors were kept clean and closed and were rarely used except to entertain special company. The Austin parlor, above the store at the front of the dwelling, was far removed from the family's main living space. It had a desk, called a library table, made of oak; two soft chairs; and a sofa. A handsome desk, in which Mama stored little red book of classics that I read, with my legs hanging from the arm of a chair, was added later.

The family album was stored there, along with a stereoscope to look at double pictures on cardboard with scenes of people and places related to WWI. And a stove to heat the room. All family pictures were destroyed along with his baby pictures, when Shanklin hid the family album in that stove to keep Mama from showing anyone his baby pictures.

An outside stairway, attached to the eastern side of the store building, ascended to a railed, covered porch, above the store porch. Two steps up from the porch, a door, with glass in the upper half, opened into the upstairs living room. The two porches stretched across the front of building.

Sportsmen who came and stayed at the Austin dwelling included: Van Campen Heilner of New York, a writer for *Field and Steam Magazine*; Albert Lyons, inventor of the automobile bumper; Henry Stellwagen of

Philadelphia, who did shingles; and a Dr. Hands, who promised sister Margie he would shoot nothing but gizzards so she would be sure to have one. Margie vied for the fowl's gizzard each time.

When I was three years old, Mr. Heilner, the first man I loved, bribed me with an orange to hold a dead waterfowl for him to take my picture in my little red boots and clothes. The picture was used for the cover of my book, *Confessions of an Outer Banks Filly*, published in 2002 by The Chapel Hill Press, Inc., of Chapel Hill, NC.

Chapter 12

Gooseville Gun Club and Hatteras Girl's Cub

Many people sought my father's help and he was contacted by some men who had come to Hatteras to hunt and fish. They wanted to build a clubhouse at Hatteras, Daddy sold land he owned; from Austin Creek to Hatteras Inlet and he stocked gun boots or waders for their hunting ventures and fishing line for their rods and reels. He functioned as their on-site representative overseeing the building of the Gooseville Gun Club.

Gooseville Gun Club

One memorable Sunday, my mother, my baby sister, and I visited the clubhouse with Daddy to see the pigeon cote on the property. His younger brother, Ernest Lee Austin, was hired as caretaker for the clubhouse. (Ernest died prematurely, October 13, 1934.)

Tom Angel cooked for the men when they came, and Alonzo O'Neal functioned as onsite caretaker. "Mr. Lon" faithfully stopped every person who attempted to go beyond the boundary of the club property and questioned them about their intentions.

After Ernest's death, Luther Lathan Austin, another of Daddy's brothers, served as the clubhouse caretaker. Luther and Tom were employees and friends, and when Tom died, he left Luther his violin; but Luther never learned to play it. Addie Neese cooked for the club members after Tom Angel's death September 23, 1937, at seventy-five years of age.

Luther would remain an employee of Gooseville Gun Club until the property was incorporated by the United States Government into the Cape Hatteras National Seashore, established in 1953. The Hatteras United States Coast Guard Station now occupies the site of the gun club house.

Daddy and the Dredge

When Albert Lyons, a member of Gooseville Gun Club, decided to make a gift of a clubhouse to the young women of Hatteras village, Daddy acquired a dredge and proceeded to fill in the stockaded lot on Slash Creek where it was to be built.

One day, when Daddy was working the dredge, Mama asked me to go tell him to come to lunch. My friend Marian Burrus and baby sister, Mona, went along with me. We passed between the parsonage and the Methodist Church and met wet sand and water. When toddler Mona began to sink into the quicksand, two scared little girls frantically pulled her to safety. I was six years old and it was 1932.

While he had the dredge in place, Daddy dredged sand for other property owners along Slash Creek and added some to his own property beyond it. I do not know just how extensive his work was.

Certainly, Slash Creek, deepened by loss of bottom, could not be waded across as I remember doing earlier. Returning from swimming at the beach, we waded through the water of the Slash to wash off our sandy feet and legs.

Daddy continued as overseer for completion of the clubhouse. He knew cement and given the directions and dimensions, he directed the building of a cement tennis court between the clubhouse and the church, which may qualify as an engineering marvel. Constructed almost one hundred years ago, that piece of cement still serves; is used as parking for the Hatteras Methodist Church and the Hatteras Health Center, where a nurse practitioner sees patients on certain days of the week.

The Hatteras Girl Club as it looked in 1941.

The clubhouse, finished in 1932, had a large central room. Outside that room, in the area toward the Atlantic Ocean, was a shuffleboard. At the front of the building were tables and chairs where the girls gathered to talk and play games. Restrooms and the kitchen opened off the central room. The kitchen door was in the middle of the back wall of the big central room.

To the left of the kitchen door, another door opened into a small room at the back southeast corner of the building. A doorway from that room opened to a stairway to the upper floor and a large community room. Two bedrooms on the west side of the building were beautifully decorated.

Mr. Lyons hired Margaret Sullivan of New York as recreation director, but her tenure was not long. Six years old, I remember having had one Saturday tap dance lesson with Miss Sullivan, "One, Two, Three, Tap!"

Local leadership for the Hatteras Girl's Club did not develop. Interest waned. Girls got married or left for school, as my sister Marjorie and others of her friends did. Care and maintenance were costly. For months, the building stood empty. Daddy and Mama kept the key, and sometimes the young people would persuade Mama to open the building and to chaperone for them to use that beautiful open space and oak floor to square danced, in a circle, rather than in fours.

Finally, Mr. Lyons decided to give the club building to Dare County and had Daddy post his intention in a newspaper.

Between 1940-1943, Dr. Crankshaw practiced medicine in Hatteras Village at the building that had been a club for Hatteras girls. He saw patients, performed surgeries, and delivered babies on the lower floor with the help of a local woman, a registered nurse. He and his wife used the upper floor for their living quarters.

During World War II, the U.S. Government commissioned the building for use of the United States Coast Guard Submarine Station.

The men, quartered in the building, patrolled the beach at night on horses, to protect our shore from intentional invasion. Their jeeps parked on the tennis court. Dead bodies sometimes washed ashore from the ships sunk by submarines active in the waters abreast of Hatteras. The glow of burning ships could be seen from the shore.

When the war ended, the weather bureau moved into the building abandoned by the U.S. Coast Guard. At least two apartments, with doors that opened toward the Hatteras Methodist Church, were made on the west side for weather bureau personnel. Huge weather balloons were released from the lawn of the former clubhouse.

Sometime after 1956, the weather bureau was moved to Buxton, ten miles north of Hatteras. The old weather bureau building, a historical site, is now a museum, returned to its original shape, size, and color.

Chapter 13

A.S. Austin Store

Andrew, cousins Crawford Austin, Charlie Ballance, and Perry Austin with Blaine Burrus for the evening gathering.

Reflecting, reviewing, and remembering, I know Daddy's love of his store never faltered, but his interest and ambition often took him beyond its doors. He hired others to care for the store so that he might be free to respond to other challenges. His ambition and foresight kept beckoning.

The Daisy barber chair had its place at A. S. Austin General Merchandise Store business over the years. It sat against the wooden wall enclosing the chimney, facing the front door of the store for a long while and was a favorite place to sit and read *The Grit*, a publication that arrived by mail on Saturday.

Several parts of the chair disappeared over the years; the original red velvet fabric for the seat and back were replaced at least twice, once with a black oil cloth covering and finally with blue denim. Daddy did the upholstering. Mama may have helped. Daddy was good with his hand. I saw him at the sewing machine at least once.

Each evening, he returned to his store to wait on customers and be with his friends, who were as regular as the clock, which shows 5:50 PM, that hung above their heads. His friends sat on the homemade benches he had constructed years before. They exchanged views and shared news.

Telephones were scarce. The U.S. Weather Bureau at Hatteras had one and A. S. Austin Store had one. Calvin Burrus, responsible for keeping the physical telephone lines, must have had a phone. The one in the store was housed in its wooden cabinet and mounted on the wall of a small room at the left front of the store where Daddy once cut hair.

Three rings signaled an incoming call for the store. When making a call on one, used a small crank on the right side of the phone to connect to a central operator. The operator connected the store phone to the right circuit. During the renovation of the building, Daddy built a pinewood telephone booth for the phone.

Austin Store received messages from New York and other places. When one was received from one of the residents at Gooseville Gun Club someone had to get in a vehicle and take the message to them and have them return the call. Sometimes, an emergency call would come to the store for someone in the village.

Uncle Fred Austin, who owned the fish house on Rollinson Creek, came each day to call Globe Fish Company of Elizabeth City to know what fish they were buying and the price they were paying. He worked for Woodley Grocery Wholesalers of Elizabeth City as well and called orders to them.

Before the renovations to the building in 1950, the room that held the telephone was used by a visiting dentist, named Woodward, and an ophthalmologist, whose name I do not know. After the 1950 renovation the arrangement of the store changed and it no longer carried dry goods and notions.

During his fifth some years as a merchant, my father learned a lot about human nature. The poem, in a homemade frame that hung on the by his office door read:

"If I knew you and you knew me/ 'Tis seldom we would disagree..."

Daddy's store stayed open to catch last minute trade and late opinions. Much good conversation went on around the stove in the wintertime. In the summer, the same location drew the usual crowd to exchange views or heated discussions.

Sometimes, when business was slow, Daddy could be found in his office at the roll-top oak desk catching up on things. That is where the man from the community found him that Saturday evening and requested credit at A. S. Austin General Store. Traditionally, customers ran their accounts from month to month and "settled up" promptly, when possible. Daddy knew the man well. They had been boys together. He asked: "Haven't you been trading with Dolph Burrus?"

"Yes, sir, I have."

Daddy did not beat around the bush. He asked, "Has Dolph turned you away because you haven't been paying your bills?"

"If I take you on and you don't pay me, I'll have to turn you away. I think the best thing for me to do for both of us is to give you this."

Daddy shifted on one hip in the swivel desk chair, reached into the pocket of his pants and handed the man a ten-dollar bill. Ten dollars would buy an ample supply of groceries for a family for a week at that time.

I was there when Daddy told Mama. He laughed after he told her. Daddy rarely laughed. He gasped for breath as he tried to finish his story. His amusement was startling.

"Do you know what he did?" He laughed again until tears came to his eyes. "He took the ten dollars I'd given him and walked out of my store to spend it somewhere else."

Daddy did not think the man meant to spend it on anything other than groceries. He saw it as a joke on himself. Finally, sober, he chuckled a little and said, "It was a bargain for all that!"

Mama and Daddy in a rare moment of merriment as Gooseville Gun Club guests

Chapter 14

My Father Romanced Boats

Daddy first owned *Cathleen* and then *J.E. Sterling*. The boats were captained by different people over the years. Recently, I found a note that Victor Ballance had once been captain of the *Cathleen*. Johnny O'Neal and Daddy's youngest brother, Horton took the boat to Elizabeth City and back for a time.

Until Highway 12 provided reliable transportation over the sandy expanse between Hatteras and Oregon Inlets, the fishing industry relied on freight boats to carry the water harvest to Elizabeth City. Returning, the boats brought back the 300-pound ice "cubes" used to ice down the fish and other seafood that was shipped to Elizabeth City on its way to northern markets.

Monroe, my father's older brother, and another man fished a boat and nets Daddy owned. His brother-in-law, Lee Peele, Beatrice's husband, fished with Monroe at one time: Josephus Willis, an another.

As owner, Daddy received a third share, as did the two who fished the nets. Daddy kept the books, sometimes tied net as he sat in the store and actively helped the operation.

Once when he and I were returning from Elizabeth City, he made a side trip to Stumpy Point, quite a distance in a direction other than toward Oregon Inlet and Toby's ferry to Hatteras Island. He went to see a man about supplying stakes for the fishing operation and the for the small girl I was, it seemed to take an exceedingly long time.

Pine or sweet gum saplings used for the stakes are driven deep into the floor of Pamlico Sound. Nets are strung to the stakes and fish collect in them overnight. Fisherman visit their nets early in the morning, empty the nets into their boat and reset the nets before taking the fish to be sold and shipped.

My Father Built Boats

Daddy loved boat building. He built three. The first one he built with the help of Irving Stowe in an unpainted building on the north side of Austin Creek, across from Gooseville Gun Club. He sold that boat, named *Ramona,* for his baby daughter, to Gooseville.

The second boat, name *Sybil* for me, was built in an airplane hangar that Albert Lyons, a member of the club, had erected for his airplane. His pilot, Dave Driscoll, flew Mr. Lyons back and forth from his northern place of residence to Hatteras. Lyons must have approved and promoted the day that Driscoll gave free airplane flights to locals. I was there, but do not remember being in the airplane.

Daddy sold the *Sybil.* While visiting Aunt Rado in Berkley and walking over the bridge between Berkley and Norfolk, Virginia, I was startled by the sight of the *Sybil* docked on the Berkley side of the river. During World War II the United States government had bought boats for use in the war effort.

The *Sybil and the Cathleen* at the Fred Austin fish-house dock in Hatteras.

The third boat, a work boat for shad fishing, Daddy built in the back yard behind the store. Mama suggested Daddy name it *Jomarsha* so the three older children would not feel excluded. *Blue Mud* may or may not have been its formal name.

My Father Piloted Boats

My first memory of Daddy piloting a boat was when he took the family to Ocracoke on the *Ramona*, to visit his cousin, Eleanor Oden, one of Uncle Dock's daughters. Her husband, Joseph Burrus of Hatteras, was keeper of the Ocracoke Lighthouse. The family lived in the keeper's quarters.

Daddy piloted a small yacht, the *Brant*, owned by Gooseville Gun Club to Elizabeth City and took Mama, Mona and me along. John Ballance and his son Linwood were also part of the crew.

During our play, when Linwood was chasing me, I fell back off a ladder inside the cabin and split my head open. No stitches needed, but I had been taken to a doctor. I do not remember how we returned to Hatteras, aboard the *Brant* or the *Cathleen*

The most memorable trip was made in 1936. Daddy captained the *Sybil* to take a boatload of children to Elizabeth City for tonsillectomies. His daughter, Mona and two cousins, Jessalyn, Fred's daughter, and Lovie, Beatrice's daughter, were ready to enter first grade. Josephine and Eliza, another of Fred's daughters, had failed to have tonsillectomies before entering school, a requirement of the era. While Mary Harlowe, Monroe's daughter, and I went had, we went along for the trip.

Mary and I had been with a whole slew of cousins in Manteo in the summer of 1932, before I entered first grade. I do not remember how we got there. Possibly Daddy took us then. What I do remember is that Maurice Peele and I were delighted to be given ice cream to soothe our sore throats.

Returning from Elizabeth City, we were in the middle of Pamlico Sound. A summer squall appeared, with heavy rain and wind. Fumes and heat from the motor on the cabin floor had children lying on the benches attached to the sides of the boat. Mama, trying to protect a child from the rain held a held a tarp as a shield and sang: "Throw out the lifeline, throw out the lifeline, someone is downing today..." - from a gospel song. Her action was a ploy to relieve tension.

Daddy guided the craft safely through the choppy water. The storm ended. We arrived at the dock, safely home. No one suffered ill effects.

Chapter 15

Movies at Hatteras -- The Pavilion and Austin Theater

Hatteras Village from the Slash Bridge and snow

Before Ellsworth E. and Leona Austin Burrus, built the Atlantic View Hotel in 1928, they lived in a home "up the road," as Kohler Drive was known. A store building sat closer to the road and to the right of their home.

It was said that Burrus owned the first car on the island and my father, the second. Both men had vision and purpose. Their relationship was always respectful and amiable, rather than competitive.

Their Pavilion, which sat in front and to one side of the hotel. Dancing was allowed there and their son Corlette climbed a wall ladder to a small projection room to show movies.

I adored Rebecca Gaskins, Colette's wife. Once I walked the marsh tussocks beyond Willie Willis' house to get to the hotel, where she and Corlette lived in an upstairs apartment at the back of the hotel. It never occurred to me to ask if I might go. Tussocks walking got me there faster than the road that wound to the left after the Slash Bridge and past Victor Ballance's home.

Beck took me with her to see *Frankenstein.* She promised to alert me, so I could cover my eyes, for the scary parts when he became a *mo*nster. I saw *Sonny Boy* with Wallace Berry and Jackie Cooper at the Pavilion with Beck.

Skating was allowed in the Pavilion after it was moved from in front of the hotel toward the ocean. Occasionally someone managed to round up a group for a square dance.

Corlette taught Marjorie piano, which has me suppose he attended school off the island. He returned to help and honor his father, as Shanklin did after finishing high school at Oak Ridge Military Academy.

My father decided to build a theater, with modern equipment and a silver screen, hoping to provide employment for Shank. Mama objected to having the theater built in the side yard. I was with her in the wash house when Daddy came to tell her something about the progress of his plan. I sensed her displeasure.

The theater roof was shingled with red and green shingles, purchased from Mr. Stellwagen's Philadelphia company, in a zigzag pattern. Sixteen-year-old Josephine sold tickets. The first movie shown was *Lady for a Day*, filmed in 1933.

Corlette taught Shank to run the projectors. His mother, Leona Austin Burrus died in 1936. The hotel was sold to Scottie and Nettie Robinson Gibson and the Burrus family, Ellsworth, Corlette, Rebecca. and their young son, Winston, moved to Norfolk, Virginia. Ellsworth died there in 1969. Rebecca outlived Corlette. Their son Winston died during 2023.

Austin Theater-circa 1942

The first movie shown at Austin Theater starred May Robson. Shank received a glossy black and white photograph of several movie stars; one was of Robson. I received an autographed one from Dr Edouard Lippe: "To my Sweetheart Sybil Dean from your movie boyfriend Lippe."

Dr. Lippe and his friend Ryland stayed with us at Hatteras one summer and into the fall. He called Mona and me "The little darlins," in derision I thought. I did not know that word then.

We may have amused him. It was during his stay with us that Mona, chasing me with a broom, broke the glass in the upstairs living room door. His gift to me of a zoology book confused me. Our dog Dobby was the only animal that interested me at that time.

Dr. Lippe was Nelson Eddie's voice teacher in New York City. Before he became famous and went to Hollywood Daddy visited Dr. Lippe. Nelson Eddie walked into the apartment, found Daddy there, thought him an intruder, and started to call the police.

After Eddy became famous, he lured Lippe to Hollywood and Lippe had a small part, as an inn keeper, in a film that starred Nelson Eddie and Jeanette McDonald. He was a movie star!

Daddy last saw him in 1936. He visited him in Hollywood after driving with five others across the country to California. While family visited, Daddy took a side trip to visit his friend. Both were victims of deformity, Lippe's due to an automobile accident. Both were overcomers. Heros!

Dr. Edouard Lippe

Besides having the theater, Shank worked in the store. He and Ruby Meekins of Avon were married in 1938 and were part of our family group. Then Mama helped them convert the front part of the house, the living room and two bedrooms into an apartment of their own. One bedroom was used for cooking and dining.

After Maurice Burrus bought the Kenfield house, they rented the small building that had been Dr Kenfield's office. When Blaine Burrus' decided to move his family away from Hatteras, Shank bought his home on the east side of Slash Creek.

Shank was eligible for the draft of World War II. He enlisted in the United States Army at Fort Bragg, December 6, 1942. After training in Joplin, Missouri, he was deployed to India as part of the U.S. Army Signal Corps, leaving me, a high school senior, in charge of his theater and to clerk in the Daddy's store.

In the picture below, Shank is on leave before he shipped to India. After Mr. Lon gave us clearance to enter Gooseville Gun Club property, we caught crabs around the end of the island, at Hatteras Inlet. Shank cooked them in a five-gallon lard can over an open fire. We ate them with zest. This picture of the five is the nearest to a family portrait that exists.

Back row: Josephine Austin Oden, Curtis and Marjorie Austin Newton.
Front row: Shank and Ruby Meekins Austin with Ramona Austin standing
behind Sybil Austin. 1943 (Photographer, Carlos D. Oden, Jo's husband)

Chapter 16

Woodmen of the World and My Father

Daddy spruced up to be photographed at my request, Circa 1938

Years after the Woodmen of the World meetings, once vital part of the community's activity, were held, those who owned Woodmen of the World insurance policies came to Daddy's store to pay their monthly premiums. My father still functioned as treasurer and corresponding secretary. When an owner of insurance died, Daddy wrote to claim the benefits for the heirs or named beneficiary. The Woodmen of the World of Omaha, Nebraska is still a vital insurance company. There may still be clubs like those once held in Hatteras Village.

During my childhood, both men and women were active in what they called lodges. They had a Woodmen of the World building and met regularly; I dreaded the foghorn sound that called them to gather. It could be heard from one end of the village to the other and I was certain the monster in that wooden box the size of Mama's trunk that stood at the top of the stairs of the lodge would eat me alive.

Vintage picture show Hatteras women, dressed in white, being taught homecare for the sick by a Red Cross nurse on the lower floor of the hall. Mama and grandmother Mogieannah were trainees. Uncle Horton extracted my grandmother's certificate from *The Bible* to show it to me. It had been filed there for more than 40 years.

When my father died in 1962, his body was returned to Hatteras from Albemarle Hospital in Elizabeth City, North Carolina for burial. Prior to funeral, his casket was housed in the old building that had once belonged to the Hatteras members of Woodmen of the World; then it functioned as the Hatteras Twiford Funeral home and Uncle Horton Austin was the Hatteras director.

My father's parents' stones. shown in the foreground of the picture below resemble cut off tree trunks. (Cement was added atop graves after 1936 storm unearthed and floated some caskets; not theirs.)

Ramona's interment, April 1912, Oden Graveyard section of
Hatteras Community Cemetery

Chapter 17

Dogs in Our Lives

Shank Austin and Dobby

Peggy, a small dog of unknown breed, mostly white in color is the first dog I remember. Shank backed out of the double garage and ran over Peggy. I witnessed the accident as a small girl. I remember the flatness of the ground and my brother's pain.

Daddy returned from a trip away from the island with a puppy to replace Peggy. He was smiling and happy with himself. I stood holding the dog in my arm. Mama did not want another dog. She disapproved and was unsmiling.

The new dog was named Snookums for one of the Black entertainers with the Robinson Medicine Show that came to Hatteras that summer. The entertainers had slept in a shop Daddy owned that sat between our house and the parsonage. Peggy had stood inside the fence and howled when Snookums sang, "Climb upon my knee, Sonny Boy….")

While we visited a Cindy Oden, Daddy's cousin, who married Glen Comer of Dobson, we were given a small white puppy, a Spitz-terrier mix. The puppy had not yet opened its eyes. We named him Dobby.

Daddy wanted to talk to Cortez Gaskins, a man with Hatteras roots, who lived in Black Mountain. The adults were talking and Mona and I were outside with Joy, their daughter. She was taller and she place our puppy on a fence post, out of our reach. Our puppy fell off the post. We thought he would die.

For the remainder of our trip back to Hatteras, Mama kept the tiny body of Dobby, which she had wrapped in a handkerchief, warm in her bosom. Daddy stopped at a drugstore to buy a medicine dropper so that Mama could feed the puppy milk.

Dobby lived for many adventures and much adoration from the family. Only Margie, our oldest sister, disliked him. Margie wanted him outside. She did not want him to mess up the house. Mona and I wanted him with us wherever we were, even in bed.

Mama was tolerant -- or did not know --we placed Dobby under the covers to warm our feet. Our bedrooms were unheated. Dobby wiggled up and contentedly placed his head on one of our arms to sleep.

He was better than a doll. He let us dress him in doll clothes and rock him like a live baby. He closed his eyes and pretended to sleep.

Once, in front of the house on the soft sand of the road, a car ran over Dobby. We were so afraid he would die. Mama propped him on pillows in a box in the living room. Perhaps she prayed for the little white bundle. Soon he was well again, following us everywhere and protecting his territory with his big bark. His breastbone seemed more prominent after that.

Once he followed the car as we were leaving on a trip. Daddy kept driving in the sand ruts, going slowly. Finally, he stopped and had us take Dobby inside the car. When we arrived at Elizabeth City, we put Dobby on the freight boat with Uncle Horton to go back to Hatteras.

When we returned home, Dobby was so happy to see us. He squirmed along the ground, made wild leaps in the air, yelping happily. Uncle Horton said, "That dog would not eat a bite since you've been gone!"

Once Dobby joined the Hatteras Methodist Church choir. He sneaked out when someone opened the door and followed Mama's scent into the church, up the aisle, and into the choir loft. Mama stooped down, scooped him up in her arms, and never missed a note. Otherwise, he might have lent his voice, as he sometimes did when she sang at home.

One day he followed Mama down the road to visit Lizzie Gaskins. Dobby tried to ignore their German shepherd. He sometimes intimidated larger dogs on his own ground, but not one. This one took Dobby's whole head in his teeth and despite the white fur ruff around Dobby's neck bit his neck deeply. Mama brought Dobby home and bandaged him up again.

Mama took care of chicks, canines, and children. Her gentle soft hands and loving care extended to other sick people who had no one else to care for them, as well.

Another day he followed me when I went to see my cousin Ruby. He tore their net screen door. It did not resist his toenails as the metal screens at our house did, Aunt Maude was so upset! I took Dobby home. Daddy may have given Uncle Nacie, a carpenter, new screen for his door.

During a bad hurricane in 1933 or 1936, I was so afraid. Dobby and I were in an upstairs bedroom. I picked him up, buried my face in his ruff, and prayed. When I started downstairs again, the water had begun to recede. I knew God heard my prayer.

Once Mona and I missed our dog and no one explained where he was. Dobby was a lover. We learned that Zilphia Austin had taken him into her house when her own small dog was in heat. We were excited when we learned Dobby was to be a daddy. Puppies! Why did no one explain to two worried little girls the absence of their pet?

I was not home when Dobby died. On his way to Norfolk or Elizabeth City, Brother Shank came by Cousin Myrtle's in Wanchese to tell me. I wanted to go home immediately. He promised to come back for me next day. Grieving, I hardly slept that night.

Mama had found Dobby by the bed. He had tried to get up to her. Mama fretted. Had she responded she might have saved his life. Dobby had been poisoned. He was six years old.

Dobby's loss was painful and my first grief experience. We would not have another dog, but Mama raised a hog named Tom and a turkey, which was meaner than sin.

Chapter 18

Andrew, the Traveler and Car Driver

My father drove a horse, piloted boats, and drove a car many miles during his lifetime. He made trips to Elizabeth City and necessary ones to Norfolk when Mama was hospitalized there. Later, he drove to western parts of North Carolina when Shanklin, Marjorie, and Josephine were in school and in 1936, Daddy drove across the United States to California.

Shanklin finished his last two years of high school at Oak Ridge Military Academy; Marjorie, her last two years at Peace College in Raleigh. Josephine attended two years at Woman's College of UNC at Greensboro and finished in June 1941 at the University of North Carolina in Chapel Hill with a degree in journalism, before taking a job with Morrison Furniture Company in High Point, where she met her husband, Clifford Curtis Newton.

Daddy, Mama, Mona and I attended Josephine's graduation from Carolina and visited Marjorie, a new mother, in High Point, North Carolina, June 1941. When we returned to Josephine's dorm, she had a message to call Shank. He was in Norfolk. Uncle Fred, two years younger than Daddy, had died of a heart attack.

Mona remained with Josephine. They went to help Marjorie with the new baby, Marjorie Elizabeth (Beth). Mama, Daddy, and I returned to Hatteras, arriving late in the afternoon.

That evening, Mama and Daddy went to be with Uncle Fred's family. Alone in that big place that was "home," is the loneliest night of my experience up to that time.

The longest drive Daddy ever made, however, was the one in 1936. That year, he drove the four-door sedan that belonged to Mama's sister, Lillian, and husband Nathan Daniels of Wanchese to Oakland, California, and back. Mama's account of that trip, and her first and only visit to Hot Springs, Arkansas, follows:

Travel Journal of Inez Daniels Austin

July 5, 1936, leaving Hatteras 3:15 PM

The ride from Hatteras to Oregon Inlet, Pamlico Sound to the left of us, the Atlantic Ocean to the right of us, required one hour and forty-five minutes of our first lap of our long, long trail -- a trail I always longed to take, but never dreamed of taking; was unbroken by any hindrance or mishap.

We stopped for a few minutes in Frisco to talk to Mr. and Mrs. Hedges and at Pea Island Coast Guard Station for water to put in a steaming radiator.

The sun is hiding behind the clouds. A recent short electrical storm, accompanied by a good shower, drove us to put our luggage inside the truck. Now on the ferry crossing Oregon Inlet, we talk with Toby Tillett about our trip.

We left Wanchese for a rainy, slow drive to Elizabeth City. We arrived, boarded the *Brant*, the Gooseville Gun Club yacht, and went to bed at 1:30 AM. So ended our first day.

July 6th -- Cooked and ate breakfast on the yacht. Went downtown shopping. Had lunch in Central Cafe. Then we all piled in -- three on the back seat and three on front seat -- and away we hie.

At 3:15 PM filling tank with gas just outside of Elizabeth City and find mileage on car: 14,754 miles.

The ride through the Albemarle section of the mainland was very pleasant. A crowd ahead. What does that mean? Oh, yes, a wrecked car to the left just off the highway. No one seems hurt, so we go.

At 8:45PM at a little barbecue stand near the WPTF Power Station, we get a sandwich, feel rather good, so we step around a bit to the radio music.

We have taken the wrong road. Yes, Sanford, not Greensboro. Oh well, we will stay here tonight.

On July 7 Bobby Burrus Cabins -- Spent a very refreshing sleep and enjoyed breakfast here. The people are kind and accommodating, 9 o'clock leaving. My goodness, we are not doing much hurrying! A nice morning sun is shining. Trees look beautiful. The land is getting hillier as we go.

Do we smell tobacco? Yes, we smell tobacco. Where are we? Winston Salem. We rode around to see the town. Then from atop the Reynolds Building, we see the surrounding country, dotted with flowers, trees, highways -- man's habitat.

We decided not to eat dinner here. Bought the makings for sandwiches and drinks, fruit and smokes (cigarettes) and headed toward Mocksville on road 158. From there into Statesville on route 66. Stopped there to change oil and have car greased, since it had been driven one thousand miles since a lubrication.

Corn, tobacco and cotton looks good to us -- there is no noticeable crop shortage in North Carolina.

Late Tuesday evening we rode through, around and over the mountains. Thrills a plenty, but with care no spills.

Along the beautiful French Broad River, mountains to the right, river to the left. Beyond that the railroad track and the mountains beyond that. Little boats chug, chugging on the river, train puff, puffing on its track. And the cars toot, tooting on the highway. On to Knoxville

At 10 PM we are very tired but soothed and refreshed after supper and shower. Then off to dreamland in lovely Irish Cut Cabins in Tennessee.

Wednesday morning, we feel so good. The service was fine. With a smile one might say and do we feel great. Had a good night's rest. On to Newport.

We see the sun rising over the mountains. Beautiful! But not more beautiful than an ocean sunrise. Different.

The land is rolling hills and valleys. Vegetation seems sparse. Lots of cows and sheep and many stands where fox chokers are being sold. They are lovely.

We got so tired last night we didn't make Knoxville. So here is where we eat our breakfast, in a Coffee Shoppe. The folks here all look very "townish" and we feel rather like we aren't a part of the setting. Guess we'll have to forget chasing sand fiddlers and slapping mosquitoes before we can adjust ourselves to changed surroundings. The girls are already looking for cowboys.

We stopped at McMinnville to get oil and have tires checked. This is a warm country. Sol is busy. Crossed Tennessee River at 5 o'clock, Central Standard Time. Our time is an hour slower than when we started. The third day is very nearly done and our chauffeur (Andrew) shows signs of fatigue. So, Brucine gets busy. You are the nurse.

July 9th Spent night in cabins beyond the Mississippi River. We enjoyed the drive last night and drove late. Memphis is such a clean, quiet city. All the folks mostly have gone to bed just to give us a chance to see the city, I suppose. Lovely homes and lots of business places but all is quiet on the river front.

Today the sun is showing God's power. So far, we have progressed along our way slowly, drinking in the beauties of nature. Rich level lands green with growing corn and cotton. As we turn a bit southwesterly cotton seems to be the principal crop.

Ah, here we are in Little Rock, Arkansas! Now we wonder where our friends the Russell's home might be. (Probably is a reference to The Reverend Leon Russell, who served Hatteras Methodist Church). These folks seem to be very industrious. Everyone is going or coming and seem bent on some purpose.

We went on to Hot Springs. Spent two hours on National Reservation Tower, near government hospital. Were shown through Buckstaff Bathhouse. (Andrew spent time here for treatment years earlier, therefore, the interest in this facility). Felt like a bath but were too anxious to see more and get on. Here is where we had two hours to wait to get a luggage carrier put on back of the car so our crowd could be able to get in and out with whole necks.

Rode out of town looking for our road seven. Missed it and rode out forty miles on seventy, which was wrong road to take us to Arkadelphia. Was directed back through town and went too far. But stopped for drinks and sandwiches. All the gang looked sore. Well, here we go anyway, four blocks back with a left, a right, a left turn through this hot, dry town. It was beautiful this morning and we had a good time. But when all were tired and cross, nothing seemed anymore.

"For the love of Mike" here is Texarkana in the late hours of the ending fourth day. What a reception! A pistol shot awoke the sleeping inmates of the car with a start. What was that? A hold up? No, just some young fellows shooting for fun. On we go, joking and laughing, thinking it would be lots of fun to be told to "stick up hands."

Spent the night in Broadway Cabins, Texarkana -- the town in three states -- a lovely, well-kept court. Beautiful lawn, flowers and trees well cared for. Such nice cabins and a refreshing shower and supper. Then off to bed.

Friday morning, we arose early and rode quite a long way before we stopped to get breakfast in a little cowboy town. We talked to lots of folks and walked around some. We thought the men would be rough looking and wild. In- stead they seemed very friendly and quiet. Yes, we all say highways are pleasant ways.

Corn and cotton, green on either side, as we pass out of northeastern part of Texas into Oklahoma. We see an occasional Indian. We might see the Wyland in this state if we knew just where.

Stopped in Bennington for gas and drinks and visited with a lovely old man who was a bit deaf. The principal crops along our way are wheat, corn, and rice. Sleek cattle and ranches here are plentiful. Land has not been so mountainous but we are on Arbuckle Mountains, rocky and almost barren.

At a cool drink stand here we stop for much needed refreshments. This has been a terribly hot day. All along we see beds out on lawns. Homes seem rather small but the outdoors sleeping are for more air, presumably.

Passed, Oklahoma State Training School on the right with well-kept lawns. Passed the dry Canadian River. Here the sand looks just like our Dare County beach sand. Passed through Norman, then into Oklahoma City, where we find oil wells and more oil wells, thicker than telegraph poles we see on our home beaches. Soil is dark and heavy. Looks as though oil would almost drip out of the topsoil.

My, it was exciting driving through Oklahoma City. Traffic was thick and everyone was in a great hurry.

The 10th day is ending. The 10th day of the month, I mean, our fifth day out.

We spent the night in nice clean cabins in Clinton, Oklahoma. Early in the cool of the morning we rode along wide stretches of cultivated lands -- for miles and miles -- on either side. In Elk City we stopped for breakfast; saw the marker of the Chisholm Trail.

Just look on the road shoulder! Daisies (gaillardia) in profusion, just like those on Gooseville Gun Club Property. Maybe those back in Hatteras were in wheat from Oklahoma that went ashore years ago.

Well, soon we will be in Texelo, the town in two states. Here it is and through we go. Stopped at an oil well to see the oil pumping operations. It was raising oil from 2100 feet below the surface; was considered a new well but had been pumping since 1923 and was still flowing freely.

On to Amarillo -- grazing lands and ranches are seen frequently. Then the scene changes to oceans of golden wheat just as far on either side as eye can see. Looking out over the Atlantic Ocean, imagining it still and gold in color, one gets a clear conception of what these wheat fields resemble.

What is the matter, Esther, did your chair break down? We stopped at Amarillo, Texas, to get chair repaired and for drinks.

Looks like we may have rain, so at the next store we'll stop and buy oilcloth to put over our luggage.

Here is the store. We bought fruit, sandwiches and plenty for a picnic lunch. We haven't had a picnic yet. Out of Amarillo 12 miles, (or 12 minutes) we had the picnic and enjoyed it quite a lot. Gathered some wildflowers, too.

We were not in the car for long after our lunch before we realized the luggage was covered none too soon. The rain ascending (descending) in torrents.

A new road ahead, clay and unpaved. Here's where we got out of our shoes and hose and plugged (plunged) out in the mud to try to help the car to stay in the middle of the road. It was slipping and sliding around so that if we stayed in, we might meet ourselves coming back.

There's an oil truck on either side in the ditch and nine more cars, this way and that. But no two heading in the same direction. We couldn't help any standing out in the rain so in we got... Nath (Nathan) looked sore seeing all that mud go in the car. But we couldn't stay in panhandle all night. We couldn't help the car much anyway. One member got her hands around luggage lashings and couldn't turn loose. The others tried to stand themselves, which was no easy job.

Oh gee! "Oh, shall we ever get out?" someone asked.

Oh, yes, this was lots of fun and were we muddy and was the car black? No, just the color of clay all over.

At ten minutes past six Saturday evening, we said good-bye to the muddy panhandle and that part of the new, broad highway of America, road (route) sixty-six. Nothing exciting is along here. Good road, sage brush, a cactus. Where are we? Oh yes, in New Mexico. Now we seem to be getting somewhere. Slept in Oklahoma last night, had a picnic and mud in Texas. Here we are in New Mexico and maybe no more bad roads.

Homes are miles and miles apart. "What's that ahead?" someone asked. New Mexico, Port of Entry, was the answer. STOP! Well, now what?

"Do you have the title of your car?"

We held our breath. We knew it was back in Wanchese. No! Lillian said, "Nez, hand me that envelope." Our hearts began to beat naturally again.

The officer, asked what he would do with us had we not had the necessary papers along, answered, "Just keep you here in San Jon until we could get a message to your capital." (North Carolina?)

We were glad we were prepared. All goes well but clouds are hovering over the mountains ahead, as we pass out of Tucumcari. The mountains are taller and more rugged. Stones are strewn all over the hill sides.

The clouds are hovering lower. The thunder is rolling, lightening flashing. No homes seem nearby. No stations. And what a night. It seems that such a storm came just at this time to help one to appreciate this rugged country. Such a picture! What wonderful thrills. The storm was terrifying because we knew there was great danger. But, oh how beautiful!

Lights are showing ahead and do we feel grateful! Santa Rosa, a little Mexican town, your hotels are over-crowded and tourists, who got in before the storm struck, are everywhere.

Found some cabins but had no pillows. We were told that in some places we would just be out of luck if we did not have bedding along. So here is where we find someone else knew more than we knew. One blanket, our zipper bag, some sweaters, a pad and rubber ring for our pillows and to dreamland we go after tense nerves have become more normal and we're bathed, fed and happy.

Sunday dawned bright and clear. So, we got up bright and early, ate a nicely cooked and served meal at coffee shop. Reports had come in that roads were impassable but we decided we didn't mind bad roads since a part of our crowd knew Hatteras banks roads. So, on we journeyed. At 7:30 AM, riding along the Peeks River, we found eight-foot culvert washed out. Boards had been laid over that. Men were already busy to help travelers. We had the road quite alone for two hours while the folks back in Santa Rosa wait for bus report about the road. The Tar Heels must see for themselves. Suppose we may be Jonahs. But know the New Mexico people will like us. Rain last night was their first in three months. At a cafe sixty-one miles east of Albuquerque, we had lunch and a nice visit with those nice friendly people. It seemed a lonely place in the desert. They made a good living, they said and their children were taken by bus to good schools. So, they were happy.

Passing through Moriarty, a typical western town and on to the green and white city that is spot of beauty in the desert. Found mountains, rock strewn. Cedars dotted all over them. All along now we see small Indian and Mexican settlements and reservations.

The country is rugged and broken -- gulches frequent, some dry bottoms, rock strewn and rough. In others, water swirling around the rocks, and over.

Look ahead. Hatteras must be here, a part anyway. There are two Hatteras names: Gaskill and Oden. Business folks, too. Advertising on the mountains' stone. Wood is scarce. Look! So, Li Mi Camps. And ahead New Mexico's cleanest, whitest city, Albuquerque.

Homes are made of native clay and stone. Beautiful trees and flowers. Lovely wide, clean streets. What a heavenly place and it is Sunday noon. People are going home from church services. Such a nice picture. Nicely dressed people. Clean town with white homes and green trees. A heavenly place!

Crossed the Rio Grande on road sixty-six and on to Gallup. Saw lots of fruit farms.

When we blow horn to pass car, the answer is a toot, toot of horn and slowing car. Quite different from our eastern travelers.

Visited Isleta (Little Island) -- Indian Pueblo and bought some souvenirs there.

Riding on to Gallup, wending in and out among the mountains, we view the Indians trying their skill at a ball game at Laguna Indian Reservation. Bought some pottery from Acoma maidens who were selling their wares from little tents and shelters by the roadside. The sun is getting low but shines on the Painted Desert and brings out nature's rich coloring.

Grants, New Mexico, another name we've heard: Hedges. My, this isn't such a big country after all! Like names, we find it all over. (Hedges was the name of a man who retired to Hatteras Island in 1930s)

There is Mount Taylor to our right, 11,390 feet. It's 4:30 PM and we are galloping through Gallup. We don't like the wild and woolly west so much. The men have unkempt hair, harsh features, and long knives in their pockets. Anyway, that Mexican food was good at Eagle Cafe and just across street a fur trader's store -- L.H. Daniels. Home again!

At 7:45 PM Arizona Port of Entry. We have already been checked through New Mexico, so a stop and wave of the hand is all here.

Rode seventy-five miles to Farrow's Auto Court, Holbrook, Arizona. Cabins were clean and comfortable. So, a nice shower and a chat with Mr. Farrow, another man having a Dare County name.

The sun is shining. "Up everyone," Andrew calls and all the sleepy heads put on smiling faces and meet the morn. Monday, 12th, yes, and still a long way from the Pacific yet.

The sun is not as high as we get started. We bought souvenir cards and stones of Petrified Forest. This is mostly level country.

At Winslow, Arizona we had breakfast, had two new tires put on car, had car washed and greased and did a bit of shopping. It was such a long wait, the ladies decided to walk on. We walked quite a distance, about a mile or more, and decided our chauffeur had taken another road and left us. We wondered what we would do. We did not have a cent with us. Guess we could get W.P.A work in the west as well as in the east.

It's 10 o'clock and there they are. Gee, it looks good to see a car stopping for us and someone in it we know! Hot walking.

On to Grand Canyon. We stopped along the way to visit caves of ancient cliff dwellers, the Apache. Wanted to gather some stones for souvenirs but could not feel right about it. The stones were too large to remove. And we didn't feel like caving in the caves by removing stones. So, we got a prickly pear pad, which we later lost, instead. Now we are moving on. Road workers.

The next stop, Winona Camping Ground and filling station. Surrounding country shows richer vegetation -- pines of good size, corn, peanuts. And here is Kit Carson Farm.

Passing over Flagstaff Mountains, we stopped at this place for gas and fruit. Then turning soon to the right on the trail to Grand Canyon on route 66, seeing to our right San Francisco Mountains, elevation 12,794 feet, highest point of land in Arizona.

The tourist camps among the pines look so peaceful and inviting. Would that we had time to spend here.

Standing by the rail overlooking the Grand Canyon, one is awed at the wonders that nature gives us in this one spot. Miles and miles of rock formation. Different shapes and colors. Ledges of rock formed so that they look like steps of every conceivable color.

The CCC are working, planting trees and making the park more beautiful. The line lying between the flat upper rocks and the dark ones with vertical structure below represent a tremendously long interval of time. The lower dark rocks were once high mountains; were later worn to flat surface. Then deposits of a great series of sediments were deposited to form more mountains. They also were eroded away. Finally, the grayish-green pebbles and sand acumen -- lasted as beach, estimated by geologists to have been five hundred million (years?) later. Here along the Colorado (River) is where we see earth in the making.

Leaving Grand Canyon on route 89, passed through Williams and Monte Carlo. Then on through miles of fenced cattle range. An old man, at whose filling station we stopped for gas and fruit, told us that the range back of his place had 60,000 head of cattle on it. Here as everywhere else, the big fish eats the little fish. This old fellow, who had depended for his living, now cannot own great herds anymore because he can't fence his range. So here is what happens. The cattle are sold to the big rancher, who can afford to fence his range.

The next town is Seligman, a small town. And now we are leaving the higher mountains behind and wending on between hills and valleys getting much level country. Here we are thinking of home. They are all peacefully sleeping because it's 12 o'clock there where our left loved ones are. And we have two or three more good hours to drive. It is only 8 o'clock with us.

The vegetation is richer now as we pass through Hyde Park. We ate our supper at Kingman; prepared for a night in the desert by oiling and greasing car; filling our thermos bottles and on again.

Everyone seems to be anxious to cross the desert, as much of it as possible, at night. They claim the Needles is the worst place we must pass. Well, here we go.

Ah! Look ahead. How did we so quickly get on mountains of such precipitous heights in such a short time? There is a sign which says put your car in second gear. My, we are thrilled and scared nearly stiff. We are afraid to even turn our heads for fear, maybe even a nose may help to send us in a nosedive down one of these steep mountain sides.

At times, the accelerator was not even in use. The brake pushed clear to the floor and it was hard to check the descent of the car at that. This has been a nerve-wracking hour and one-half and aren't we glad it isn't going to be like this all the way? The drop was so steep.

After crossing the Rio Grande River, we felt very tired. Our nerves had been so tense. But decided to ride on a little longer. Nearly everyone is dropping to sleep.

Here is where we will stop. The road is deserted. Everyone has pulled off the road -- trucks, cars, vans, etc. We will do the same.

The two men -- Andrew and Nathan -- of course were left in the car. The four ladies, with one blanket, foxed around on the desert the two hours the men slept. Ah, but it was nice and cool. Down we spread our blanket and down we go.

The wee little noises of the night, nothing but sky and desert sand around us banished sleep from our eyes. Not a place could we find to rest for long. New noises! And up the party of four jump to find a new, better place. No sleep -- just talk and laughter.

We performed meager ablutions from our thermos jug. Slicked our hair but did not powder our noses. Of course, we didn't dress. We foxed around in our clothes so we got going again. Besides there isn't much chance to hide out here, even from our own party.

In the early morning hours, we are covering miles and miles of sand, sage brush and cactus, the only visible vegetation. The hills seem to be a darker soil than we've been seeing for past few days.

Here is the Agricultural Registration Station, but we must get to it to get inspected. It was not such a bad ordeal. We looked rather like tramps. By the time two or three bits of clothing lying around in car were seen by the agent, he must have decided we were quite harmless. And let us go on.

First, he had to know some facts: who owned the car? Hometown of party. Where we were bound. Who were we going to see? How long we intended to stay. If we had money enough to take care of our needs. I began to think we'd have to call Raleigh, North Carolina and get our birth certificates. Now, would we not have been in a great pickle for when we were born, they did not have birth certificates? Oh well, we got on fine. Some people even get their hat bands searched.

In Barstow, not long after G. S. experiences, we comb our hair, powder our noses and get breakfast. Aren't we swell looking spectacles to be in California? And on to Los Angeles and Hollywood. Still on sixty-six road.

Palms are dotting the land on either side of the highway. We passed over San Bernardino Mountains, the highest in California. These mountains are green -- beautiful after so much desert sand. The roads are smooth and wide -- a beautiful drive.

Stopped for drinks at Verdemont Stores. Drove through St. Bernardino. On to Pasadena. Here we saw orange groves and tropical palms. Great groves of grapes, as far back from road on both sides as one can see. Towns are more frequent; hardly pass one and get speed up before down we go to twenty-five speeds again.

Here we are in Los Angeles. It's about 11:30 o'clock. This is the 11th day out. Now the next thing to do is find Dr. Lippe. Andrew is determined to see him and say HELLO before we get to rest on this day. We've spent two hours hunting. I know we went around the hill on which his home rests two or three times and no Troy drive visible. We are all mad, hot and hungry so we give up the search for a while. We'll get settled, some lunch, a shower and some sleep.

Later in the PM Andrew left us and found Lippi, who came for us with Mr. Ryland to go over to dinner with them and Mr. Cameron. Which we did and enjoyed same.

Esther and Brucine went to town, missed this treat, and had to be found at bedtime. They say they weren't lost. Maybe not. But they gladly came in and to bed. So ends the day and tonight we rest in Hollywood.

Rode around and viewed the city. Thursday morning, we called on Lippi to bid him adieu and shook hands with Dick Powell, who was at Doc's place for his voice lesson.

Leaving we took road along coast to Oakland. Winding among the hills and orange groves it is plenty warm. Sunny California is right hot a plenty when our road swings us away from the cool, inviting Pacific.

Passing through Camarillo, California after a 15-mile detour, we feel the welcome sea breeze on our faces. This is really the most beautiful country we have driven over since we entered California. On either side of the road are palms, cedars, fruit trees, peas, peanuts and flowers. Geraniums grow as profusely here as water bushes on the Atlantic coast. Much of it is higher than our heads and used for hedges -- all the colors. One complete riot of color! Oleanders, too, are beautiful -- pink, rose and red.

In Ventura, a town of flowers, here is where we see the Pacific Ocean for the first time. We knew before, when we were close to it, by the cooler atmosphere. Driving over the peaceful rock-strewn ocean drive, on to Oakland. The smell of the ocean and the feel of the ocean seems so refreshing after eleven days with no sight of the sea. This is beautiful smooth road. Mountains to the right, ocean on the left. Santa Barbara nestles close beside the sea.

A few more miles on ocean drive, then the road circles away and again we are climbing mountains -- through Lompoc, Santa Maria, San Luis Obispo, Santa Margarita and Atascadero. Who knew Mr. Banister Davis lived here? There's his name, anyway -- B.H. Davis, Atascadero, California and not Wanchese, North Carolina.

The country now begins to stretch out a little more flatly through El Paso de Robles (Paso Robles, now), San Miguel, and Salina. These are little mission towns -- San Ardo, San Lucas. Night begins to shut in and no more recordings.

Everywhere the towns had all their tourist homes, auto courts and hotels filled and no place for weary North Carolinians. So, another night we rest thus: Lillian, Nathan and Andrew in car; Esther and Brucine with that poor old blanket in a filling station rest room. I spent the remainder of the night talking and visiting with the filling station operator. He was glad of company. When I started in, he thought I was a hold-up maybe. He unleashed his dog and went for his gun.

I said, "Put up your gun, young man. Come here, Sheep." The dog came. I just stumbled on the right name, or else there was friendship in his heart for a weary traveler. The young man and I had quite a nice visit.

We left early and barged in on my brother's family at 6 o'clock in the morning. Was Frieda surprised!

Most of us went to bed. I plugged in between Tom and Dick and got quite a good snooze between the warm, little six- and eight-year-olds. I did not wait to see what the others were going to do. I was too sleepy and cold. That sounds funny too because all day we had warmth a plenty.

Now for a four-day visit. Lillian takes up her old job at sewing machine, so feels very much at home. Esther is the house cleaner. Brucine and Nathan help each other with the dishes. I am the laundress. Frieda is a good cook, so no one tries to take her job.

I'm crazy about Cassie's family. (Sisters Lillian and Inez and brother Cas were together for the first time since he left home as a young man, possibly during World War I.) In fact, we all are. Dainty little Barbara, golden haired, blue-eyed ten-year-old. Mischievous Tommy, eight-year-old, blonde too. Dick so tender-hearted he cries when he sees Shirley Temple in *CAPTAIN JANUARY*. Little Marge, two years, nice hello baby and okay. She had measles, too! Now wasn't that just terrible? And it wanted to be so jolly and sweet.

Friday morning Cas came home, was surprised and seemed happy to see us. He talked about old times when we were all kids home together. Lots of little things he remembered that I had forgotten.

We went to see two pictures. Some of them did a bit of shopping. Andrew went back by plane to Hollywood where he spent his four days with Dr. Lippe, Ryland and Cameron -- saw lots more than we did. But we enjoyed our visit very much with our loved one, Cas. Are we glad we found 2162 38th Avenue!

With 3,583 miles behind us, on July 21 at 10 o'clock leaving. Cassie's little family wave us adieu, as we start our way homeward.

(To *preserve form and language, italics and parenthesis are used sparingly to help those unfamiliar with the places, people and events of the travelers' lives to understand the manuscript.*)

Shank, Marjorie and Josephine were at home, and Grandpa Wheeler had agreed to stay with them. I am not sure where Mona stayed. I was with Aunt Rado in Berkley, Virginia, in a big white two-story house on Main Street, with a chinaberry tree on the right side of the house. Years later I heard Jo remark: "Grandpa didn't stay beyond a few days. We were too noisy for him. He went back home."

Chapter 19

Two Accounts of the 1936 Hurricane

Mama's account

Hatteras, North Carolina -- September 17, 1936

All day the storm has threatened. Radio reports warn us to move out of the storm area. They have no concept of knowing how slim our chances are of making a single move to save our lives! The only thing we can do is open our homes to strangers within our storm-closed gates.

The people who live nearer the shore may move nearer the center of the beach land to homes that are no safer perhaps than those right along the sound or ocean front. One little pitiful mile is the width at the widest point that separates us at this very moment from a very uncertain end.

There is one thing more we can do. We can keep on praying that a Heavenly Father will help us to be sane and sensible at this time and help us to be brave. He calmed the storm on the wind-tossed Galilee. He can do the same today.

Or are we so sinful that we must be shown the power through the elements of a Father's mighty hand?

We hope with every passing moment that the intensity of the storm may lower. We have been given by last report a slim hope that the storm may veer out to sea. Perhaps the land will not get it quite as intensely as we now fear.

May the hand that rules us all wave a gentle wand over the troubled waters and still their tempestuous tossing?

How relieved each heart -- how grateful -- should the wind quietly lower and no damage come to us and our poor earthly possessions.

The last report says 11:30 is the time set for the most dangerous hour of the storm at this point. We wait with bated breath, hoping against hope that we may not get it so terribly bad here. The tide is over the land, still rising higher and higher.

The Coast Guardsman reports by phone that he is being rocked to sleep in the tower as he watches. They have seen so many storms, so they seem unafraid.

At 12:30 the water is now fourteen inches deep in the downstairs rooms. We have the piano twenty-four inches off the floor, also a davenport on two chairs (wooden). (Sewing) machine is on the desk, refrigerator on boxes, Victrola and upholstered chairs on the tables.

The wind is still strong and flurries seem to indicate that it is increasing in velocity.

Mr. Poe (Rev. John Poe) has gone to bed, also, Shanklin. Decatur (cousin) and Josephine look like ostriches on their nest, lying on couch about halfway up to the side of the wall. Mr. Marion Holland (Hatteras school teacher) in another corner on davenport, on a high perch. Andrew sits on a highchair on first stair step, feet propped on second step. I am sitting on a stool, water sloshing up under same.

My Version of the Hurricane of 1936

The water kept getting higher and higher, up to the second step of the stairway. I went to the bedroom above the living room. My faith was young and my knowledge of the Bible, elementary. I missed knowing of God's promise with a rainbow, that the earth would never again be destroyed by water. I took Dobby into my arms and cried into the neck fur of our white-terrier-spitz mixed dog. We did not have Noah's ark. I was so afraid.

The wind velocity gusted to one hundred miles an hour; the railing atop the U. S. Weather Bureau blew off; and the "window light" at the top of the inside staircase at the back of the upstairs hall, blew in and the wind driven rain drenched us as we tried to cover the window with cardboard.

The cedar shake roof, which usually kept out the water, was water soaked by the onslaught of the hurricane. Every available pot, pan, or bucket sat around on beds and floors of the upstairs bedrooms beneath the dripping ceilings.

Many homes, and the Northern Methodist Church, in the southern part of the village, washed off their foundations. Part of the fence that went around our front yard washed out of the ground.

Sister Jo and cousin Wheeler went to take pictures of the damage after the storm. One picture showed the freight boat *Cathleen* atop racks where nets were hung to dry.

When the tide began receding, people knew to grab brooms and begin sweeping the last of the tide and sludge out the doors. Dried sludge is dreadful to remove. Then the floors were rinsed with clear water from the cistern, over which the tide had washed and contaminated our water supply.

The bathtub had been filled full of water before the tide came. That water would last a short while for the lavatory and commode, for bird baths and infrequent flushing! Briefly, water from the cistern could be used for cleaning, but it was imperative to empty the cisterns of the contaminated water, to clean them with household bleach and hard scrubbing, to ready them for the blessed, expected rain.

To prevent an outbreak of typhoid fever, everyone needed to be vaccinated. We children lined up at the appointed hour on the lawn outside Dr. Kenfield's two room, small white office building, next to his new home, built on the west bank of The Slash.

His old home, situated behind Charles Styron's from ours, had burned down. Rumor was that a hot iron, left on the ironing board, did it. More than likely, it was one of Dr. Kenfield's lit cigarettes. He smoked incessantly. The nicotine from his Camel cigarettes had turned the fingers of his right hand dark yellow, and his clothes reeked of tobacco smoke.

Dr. Kenfield had another responsibility for the village. He was the village magistrate, the only law authority the village had. However, Mrs. Theresa Rollinson signed my birth certificate in 1926, and different local men signed, as undertakers, death certificates.

Fresh rain usually follows a hurricane, but not always. When the rain delays, mosquito larvae use the salt water to breed. Their bite hurts more than that of the freshwater mosquito.

Daddy had a pump point placed in our front yard under the gnarled live oak tree, which watched over that part of the island for more than a hundred years. The ground water was hard. Even soap made from household grease and Red Devil Lye would not lather in it. That water would not help wash clothes.

In 1936 the rain did not arrive as expected and laundry piled up for everyone. Some kind and gracious individual drove a pump point low enough on the old dipping vat hill to find fresh water. One Monday morning, Mama joined other village women to do laundry there. I was one of the small children there with their mothers. We helped spread handkerchiefs and other small articles, like wash cloths, on the low-growing bushes to dry.

Daddy stops driving

By the time Mona and I were away at school, Daddy was no longer driving. Arthritis in his hips had caused his legs to cross at the ankles. For ten years Daddy depended on others, particularly his nephew Wheeler

Ballance, to drive him where he needed to go. (Wheeler had worked for him in the store years earlier.)

Daddy had begun to collect family history related to property he claimed, and Wheeler helped "Uncle Ander" by driving him to visit those who might help him unearth the truth regarding property lines of the area he was claiming on the beachfront next to decommission Durant Coast Guard Station.

Chapter 20

My Father's Employee

After I graduated from Hatteras High School in June 1943, I became a paid employee in Daddy's store. I did not need to be told what to do, or how to do it. I had grown up going in and out of the store -- entered through a door from our downstairs living area- and had worked there weekends and summers. I knew from observation and practice what was expected of me.

Once, after an encounter with a disgruntled customer, I had Daddy remind me that the customer was due respect, was not to be challenged. "The customer is always right."

First thing each morning, I swept the floor. Store traffic was manageable. Toward week's end it became a bit more demanding on Saturdays when weekly grocery orders were filled and delivered. Daddy tended the trade when I was away on delivery. He was there to answer questions and do things I could not do, i.e., cut window glass. My father was a patient man.

During the week, in slow times, while waiting, I wrote letters. I crocheted and did embroidery between customers. Sometimes I sat in Daddy's old barber chair and read to wait.

I helped myself to Daddy's stamps, stored in the top drawer of his desk to mail all those letters I wrote, even to beaus and the local lads serving in the several military branches during World War II.

One day Daddy confronted me. He smiled when he said, "I notice you are using a lot of my stamps."

Until then I had never bought my own stamps. It was time to reevaluated my status. My weekly salary of fifteen dollars was quite generous, considering I did not pay for food or shelter and as my parents' dependent did not pay taxes or Social Security from my earnings. Readily I saw that the cost of my considerable correspondence was indeed my responsibility. Thereafter, I purchased my own stamps.

Chapter 21

My Father and Durant Life Saving Station

Durant Life Saving Station, built in 1878-79, figured prominently in Daddy's life, early and late. The station, first named Hatteras Life Saving Station, was renamed Durant in 1883.

1890 Picture of Durant Life Saving Station where Wheeler Austin served.

February 12, 1879, Zorababel G. Burrus was appointed its first keeper and was responsible for choosing the six surfmen to man the oars on the boat to serve under him. Homer W. Styron became keeper when Burrus was transferred o Gull Shoal Station in 1904. Styron chose William Wheeler Austin as one of his surfmen.

Wheeler was already in service when he registered for the registered for the World War One draft in 1915. He had been in the U.S. Life-Saving Service when it and the Revenue Cutter Service merged to become the United States Coast Guard in 1915. He served for a total of twenty-seven years.

General Billy Mitchell and Airplanes

General Billy Mitchell arrived at Hatteras in 1923 to assess his belief that airplanes could sink ships. His airplanes, his pilots and men who cared for them were quartered at Durant.

Before they arrived, a landing field had to be prepared for the airplanes on the ground south of the Durant United States Coast Guard Station. The government hired men of the village and requisitioned their horses, carts, and wagons. Eight-year-old Shank Austin objected to anyone other than himself driving Old Deck and the wagon. Therefore, Shank became an employee of the United States Government, hired along with men of the village to prepare a landing field for General Billy Mithcell's airplanes.

A photographer with Mitchell took pictures of the activity of the men and airplanes on the field south of Durant Life Saving Station. The photographer took many photos of the people of the village scenes. One shows the new schoolhouse, scaffolding not yet removed.

The day of the bombing of a ship from the air off Hatteras, the whole village turned out for a picnic at Durant. Newspaper men and others came to watch and to be part of that historic day.

In 1937, Durant Coast Guard Station was decommissioned and put up for auction. Daddy bid two hundred dollars. It was believed he received the station because the property on which it say had originally belonged to his ancestors.

My father sold Durant to Albert Coates, a law professor at the University of North Carolina in Chapel Hill. Coates' wife, Gladys, stayed with us one summer as remodeling began at Durant. A porch was added to the station boathouse at that time.

When the Coates couple changed their mind about having a home at Hatteras, the property reverted to my father. Daddy must have held the mortgage.

More later about Durant Lifesaving Station.

The summer of 1940, Mona went with Mama and Daddy, sister Josephine and her friend Donald Mann to Green Island Gun Club, which Daddy owned at the time. I never visited Green Island. Before I could, Daddy sold the club to Mr. Sam Jones of Ocracoke.

He sold a lot abreast of Durant Motor Court to Joseph Massoletti, a New York restauranter. Monies from the sale of these two properties gave Daddy the funds he needed to rebuild the store and living quarters in the village.

Chapter 22

The Rebuilding of Austin Store and Dwelling

He planned to raise the heavy structure above the tide depth of the 1936 hurricane and needed enormous concrete blocks to support the larger building he envisioned. To raise the structure and to rebuilt was a formidable undertaking. Though begun in 1943, the house was still torn apart in the spring of 1946 when Don Skakle arrived to visit me. Partitions were missing to enclose the bedrooms above the store. The kitchen had only half a floor.

Sybil Austin and niece Beth Newton, in the homemade swing Circa 1943

The front door of the living quarters could be reached by walking across a board from the front steps. That summer, as my friend Marian Burrus and I returned from the recreation hall where we went dancing and socializing, the young man with Marian mis stepped and ended up under the house.

The store area was enlarged by the width of the shed and an addition was added over a basement, placed where the store porch had been. The space included what had been Mama's sewing room. Less living space remained. Since the stairway was now placed inside the living room area, on the wall where the coal heater once sat, the living space was reduced still move.

The front store porch remained. The porch above it was enclosed under the new hip roof to become two adjoining bedrooms for a front apartment. When finished, there were four efficiency apartments on the west side of the building on the upper level above the store. The old roof had to be thrown out the attic windows.

The Rural Electrification Act of 1936 had been initiated at Hatteras. Daddy no longer needed to have two Kohler motors housed in the back end of the wash house, to provide light for Austin Theater and the house and store. He did not need an engine house for the water pump that sat at the west end of the store porch. The new store basement held the water pump.

Pappy on the fence he hurdled to enter the store after closing the door from store that again opened into the living room area to satisfy Mama.

Chapter 23

Happenings of June 1950

Inez, Andrew, and Ramona Austin, Mable Skakle, and Beth Newton on the steps of the apartment house on Blandwood Avenue in Greensboro, N.C

June 1950, Mama and Daddy came to Greensboro to attend Mona's graduation from Woman's College of UNC in Greensboro, a week before his hip surgery at Duke Hospital in Durham. They would also attend the ceremonies at Chapel Hill, when my husband, Don and Virgil Wilson, the man Mona was to marry the following week, graduated from the University of North Carolina, the next day.

My husband's parents came from Waltham, Massachusetts for Don's graduation.

While Don had been finishing school – he was a year behind me- Eddie and I lived in the same apartment house, in a different apartment, as sister Marjorie, her husband Curt, and their daughter, Beth. I had been hired by the manager, Banks Kerr, of Leggett-Rexall Drug Store on Elm Street in Greensboro the October before.

We gathered on the step of the apartment house on Blandwood Avenue for pictures before leaving for Chapel Hill. In Chapel Hill we gathered at the new Morehead Planetarium for more pictures.

Daddy had not been able to drive a car for ten years, due to the crossing of his legs at the ankles, due to his hip. Arthur Godfrey, famous radio personality, had had a successful hip replacement, something new and wonderful for those in need. Daddy decided to gamble his life for a new hip. He sold all his General Motors stock to pay for his operation. We were apprehensive, due to his heart condition.

Monday, June 5, 1950, he entered Duke Hospital. He would miss Mona and Virgil's wedding ceremony on June 7th.

He did very well and in the months ahead, with a new hip, he began his new life. He used two crutches, advanced to two canes, then to only one. Finally, slim and spare, he needed no help at all and bought himself a blue and white Chevrolet four door sedan. He was able to drive.

Chapter 24

Building Durant Motor Court

Daddy, the Contractor

Wearing weary grey trousers,

A seamy shirt, and a straw hat

To shade his eyes from the

Hot August sun, he half-sat,

Half-leaned on the edge of

A cement step, watching.

His hired men shovel sand.

From the back of the red

Pick-up truck. His creased brow

Indicated the labor of his busy mind.

Planning the next phase

Durant Life Saving Station of 1878 and as it looked when swept into Pamlico Sound by Hurricane Isabel in 2003.

With both feet flat on the ground, Daddy felt empowered and began to develop the Durant Coast Guard Station property. Cape Hatteras National Seashore was getting ready for its s official establishment, which would be January 12, 1953. He foresaw the need for more and better accommodations for the people who would come to the seashore park.

In the station building he planned two apartments, one upstairs and the other downstairs.

The entrance remained the same and served both. The upstairs needed little change. The boat room would be the large living area of the downstairs apartment and the cart shed on the east side of it would accommodate a bedroom and a bath, where the old clawfoot bathtub from the *Deering* was placed.

The separate kitchen building became a cottage and Daddy drew plans for a long building with two separate rooms on the eastern end for overnight guests, as well as three apartments. The apartments faced toward a cement court, across from the cottage.

Durant Motor Court was the first ready to welcome those guests attracted to Hatteras by the Cape Hatteras National Seashore Recreational Area.

*Family Christmas dinner at the newly remodeled Durant Coast
Guard Station boat house, 1953.*

Shanklin and Josephine and their families made their homes at Hatteras. Marjorie, Ramona, and I and our families from "Up State," as Daddy called it, were home for Christmas in 1953. Daddy suggested we have Christmas dinner at Durant Motor Court that year. So, we assembled our food, which had been prepared elsewhere, in the old boat house area for our holiday meal.

Daddy may have intended to share stories from his youth related to his father's twenty-seven-year service at Durant and to share his vision for the future of the motor court. He did not press his case. The demands of small children, three of whom were babies; gathering the food together; and the meal itself made it a day to remember. Daddy gave each of his children a hundred-dollar bill, equivalent to more than one thousand dollars today.

Shanklin and Ruby managed and ran Durant Motor Court. They built another, next to it on a lot of Daddy gave Shanklin. Aptly, he named it General Mitchell, it was built on the ground where Billy Mitchell's men and airplanes had temporarily camped in 1923, next to the Seagull Motel, owned by Sister Josephine and husband Carlos Oden.

Eventually, Daddy "sold" Durant Motor Court to Shanklin with a note for forty thousand dollars, which, after five years of grace, he began to pay each of his four sisters one thousand dollars a year for ten years.

These payments and a portion of the property, which he claimed, was our inheritance. The property was under litigation. Heirs of John Phipps of New York claimed the same ground. The closing of the will could not be made until the court case was resolved.

Daddy had engaged Attorney McCown, on contingency, to defend his claim for an heir's portion of the said property. The fight for ownership continued beyond Daddy' s death. Twice the courts decided in our favor Finally, Shank and Attorney McCown were ready to complete the business of filing my father's will and the five children and Attorney McCown to receive their share.

Had the lawyer not questioned our father's will that gave all condemnation monies related to the total oceanfront of that property to Shanklin, I never would have questioned it.

My brother Shanklin and I became estranged. When Josephine said, "Sybil, it could have been that way." I knew somehow that that is exactly what Daddy meant to do and it was okay.

My Brother - The Years the Locust Ate

Today I imagined you on your knees,

Extending your arms to me-

As I toddled toward you and your smile.

When I was two and you were twelve.

It must have been like that.

When did you stop smiling at me?

Why were you sometimes unkind?

I tried to win back your love

Misunderstandings separated us.

I grieve for those lost years.

You must have loved, because you cared..

Neither knew the art of reconciliation.

You died, unaware I had flown from Florida,

Driven four hours alone to ask your forgiveness

To sa y to you: "I love you, Brother."

Replacing a windshield wiper delayed me.

You never saw again the face

Your angry words disclaimed.

My consolation is that in Our Savior's

Love we will reclaim the years the locust ate - Joel 2:25

Chapter 25

Daddy Took Care of His Own

September 1954 Mable Skakle, Don, Eddie with Buster Brown, Sybil and Andy Skakle in front of the Durant Motor Court apartment.

In late August 1954, my husband Don collapsed on a tennis court at Greensboro Country Club. During a three day stay at the hospital, no physical reason explained his collapse. He rejected the suggestion of his physician friend and tennis student for a psychiatric evaluation. Don was too physically and emotionally exhausted to assume teaching at Aycock Junior High School that fall. Daddy offered Don the store at Hatteras.

Our move to Hatteras followed closely the devastation of Hurricane Carol on August 31, 1954. We moved into one of the two-bedroom apartments of Durant Motor Court. Sand still covered cement parking lot. Brother Shanklin, aboard a tractor, labored day after day, pushing sand back to cover the black-brown peat beneath Hatteras Island exposed by the storm.

When it was time to winterize the motel, Daddy insisted we move into Hatteras village with him and Mama. Sensing my displeasure, Mama reminded me that she liked it no better than I. It was her space! Yet she accepted me and mine.

My mother was a saint! No, she was a teacher. She taught third grade in that school across the road where Eddie, our oldest, began first grade. It helped her that I had been there to keep the house while she taught school.

Clifford Dwight Skakle, born at the Cape Hatteras Health Center in Buxton October 26, 1956, and Pappy became great friends. Pappy responded to Cliff's requests to ride in the car with him.

We left Hatteras in 1958 to return to Chapel Hill for Don to attend graduate school and become Carolina's varsity tennis coach. Mama and Daddy, alone in that big dwelling, again had the responsibility of store, apartments, and yard again. Mama began to take a new interest in cooking for the two of them.

At the University we sponsored a young graduate student, Meckinley Scot from Assam, India and invited him to go with us to Hatteras that summer, 1959, to visit Mama and Daddy. They welcomed us and him with their usual warm hospitality and unfailing love. Cliff happily found himself again with his beloved Pappy.

When the island was separated by the Ash Wednesday storm of 1962, Mama came out of retirement to teach in Avon until the inlet was closed, returning home for weekends.

Alone, in a way they had never been before, they began to appreciate one another more. Mama's heart was warmed when Daddy called her 1910-1911 college picture: "My Queen Elizabeth." His gift to her of a stuffed bunny for Easter both embarrassed and delighted her. Love bloomed afresh for these two.

In the evening after supper, they took a ride to check the number of cars at each motel in the village. Daddy drove and stopped Mama to pick up bottles, for their monetary value and because it improved the look of the landscape, Mama's passion.

Before leaving for what would be his final visit to Albemarle Hospital and his last trip away from the island, Daddy wrote a letter to his children. He did not expect to come back home.

Shanklin went back and forth from Hatteras to Elizabeth City during his stay. Margie, suffering from multiple sclerosis, had to return home to Greensboro. Josephine remained by his bedside. Mama, Aunt Beatie, his sister, and I were in a motel across the street from the hospital when he died, Daddy left us, late Sunday afternoon, October 7, 1962. He was seventy-two years.

Pappy's Death

Sybil Austin Skakle

After the viewing we sat on the steps of the funeral home at Hatteras.

Needing to explain grief and loss to our six- year- old son
I pulled him close.

"Pappy was old and tired," I said.

In the following days I became the bereaved child struggling to
find my place

Without the father on whom I depended for security and safety for

For thirty-six years

Chapter 26

The Woman Who Survived Him

Mama came to Mona and me when each baby was due, to help us and to attend summer school. She elevated her teacher's certificate as high as possible without a college degree. At seventy-five, she enrolled in Carolina to obtain the college degree she so coveted, even though she was no longer teaching.

Modern Civilization and mathematics foiled her and her failing health required her withdrawal. Back home at Hatteras, she attended classes at Cape Hatteras School. She learned to type and took classes in art. She had taught there, beginning in 1953, until her retirement. She taught the kindergarten class at the Hatteras United Methodist Church.

Hatteras Teacher Feted At Family Surprise

THE NEWS+OBSERVER
MARCH 3, 1964

MRS. ANDREW AUSTIN

By FLORENCE KING

Mrs. Inez Daniels Austin has seldom been out of touch with children in her 75 years.

On aSturday night her five children and their families honored the Hatteras native and former school teacher at a birthday party at the Holliday Inn in Raleigh.

The widow of Hatteras merchant Andrew S. Austin served in the public schools for more than 25 years. She temporarily retired from the classroom to raise her own children, but she still retained her interest in teaching through her church school and as chairman of her local school board.

She resumed her career and her studies when her family was grown, teaching until her retirement from the Dare County schools at the age of 68.

"However, my retirement didn't last long due to the famous 'Ash Wednesday storm' in 1963," she explains.

When Hatteras Island was cut in two by this holocaust, Mrs. Austin volunteered as an emergency teacher, serving the remainder of the school year at Avon, on the northern portion of the island.

"I taught in an emergency capacity for the whole of the following year at the Cape Hatteras school," she recalls.

Mrs. Austin's latest impressive achievement?

She is working toward a bacheolor's degree in Education at Carolina.

Celebrating Mrs. Austin's birthday with her were her children and their families, Mr. and Mrs. Andrew S. Austin Jr., Mr. and Mrs. Carlos Oden, Mr. and Mrs. Curtis Newton, Mr. and Mrs. Donald Skakle, and Dr. and Mrs. Virgil A. Wilson.

Twenty days before Mama's death, we celebrated her 79th birthday at Mona and Virgil's home in Greenville, North Carolina. Mama entered the hospital ten days after her birthday and died March 23, 1969.

That Last Visit with Mama

Brother Shanklin had been there the week before and

commented on the peacefulness of Mama's room at

Polk County Hospital in Greenville, North Carolina

Early Friday morning Sister Mona telephone.

Thursday was a good day for Mama,

Now having slipped into a coma, she was in her.

Final hours. I needed to come right away.

Driving to Greenville alone, I remembered

Leaving her last Sunday afternoon to return home.

"I wish you didn't have to go," she said.

"I do too. But I'll be back soon," I replied,

fighting tears, hoping we would talk again.

"The medicine makes me so lazy," Mama said.

"I waste all my time sleeping."

Like her, to regret infertile hours.

Sisters Jo and Mona with her when I arrived.

Multiple sclerosis kept Marjorie from being there.

"Sing to her," Mona said. "She begged for songs all day yesterday."

Mama, visiting the sick and dying sang.

To comfort and encourage them.

With a lump in my throat, I began to sing:

"Each step I take, my Savior goes before me..."

And struggled to recall other songs to sing to her.

Together, sitting on the piano stool at home

She and I often played and sang together.

That evening, Mona brought me the biggest,

wettest hamburger I ever ate.

All day Saturday Jo and I sat beside her bed.

Sometimes it sounded like she moaned,

"Help me." Maybe it was not so.

Early Sunday morning she quietly slipped away.

I turned to search for Josephine,

Who had turned and sought the arms of

The nurse who had entered her room.

Twenty-two years later in Kona, Hawaii, on

a porch overlooking the cobalt blue Pacific-

as my husband Lee and I prepared to fly

back home to await Lee's cancer death-

Jo explained "I'd already grieved so much-

Had shed so many tears."

I had thanked God when Mama slipped free.

I did not try to explain to Jo my need for

her arms to hold and comfort me.

Because Mama's arms no longer could.

Her will left the dwelling which held both home and store to me with provision for paying the other heirs like those Daddy had made for Shank and Durant. After a period of grace, I was to pay my siblings a yearly increment until they were paid the full amount due them. Though the value placed on the property was minimal, it was enormous for Don and me. We dreaded debt and knew little about finance, about buying and selling property.

Brother Shanklin said, "The best thing you can do is sell the place."

We did not sell. We spent our sweat and tears every vacation working to improve the property, even before the property was official ours. We were its slaves. It owned us.

We had a new roof installed and had the place painted golden yellow. No one liked the yellow, except me. Mama had begun to have it painted flamingo pink. Probably no one except Mama liked to see it in color.

Whan my husband died in 1980, I was ready to make the final payments to my siblings for the Hatteras property. We never considered taking out a mortgage to pay for the property! Would I, were I faced with the same debt today? Probably .

It would be 1984, before Josephine, administrator of Mama's will, and I were ready to complete the transaction that would make it mine.

Our oldest son Donald Edmund Skakle, Jr. had spent every summer with Grandmother Inez at Hatteras during his college years, working as a mate on one of the fishing charter boats. As soon after graduation as he could, he returned to Hatteras. When he did not get a teaching position he requested, he bought a boat and became a fisherman. In 1984, the deed to the house was given to him for his promissory note to me for its purchase.

Improvement made since 1984 have added to its attractiveness. Eddie says," I love living in Pappy's house. I pay taxes for the privilege."

Life has taught him, as it has me, we own nothing. We pay for the privilege of accepting responsibility for tangible things that own us.

The business he conducted as A. S. Austin Company did well and required concerted effort for his wife Gail and him. They now lease the store, which continues to do well, but still have the four apartments over the store that they rent and maintain.

An Artist's View of A. S. Austin Company and dwelling circa 2008.

A.S. Austin Company decked out for Christmas.

Chapter 27

The Early Oden Family

John C. Odin (1792-1873) claimed to have been shipwrecked three times on Hatteras Island, once when only a cabin boy. Perhaps it was then that he floated ashore on a pork barrel or one holding rum. The contents of the barrel depend on who is telling the story.

Who found the boy? Where did he stay until he got back to his ship, or to his home? Perhaps William Stringer Stowe found him and took him home, where he came to know the family and a little girl named Lovie Alice (1799-1870), seven years younger than he.

In 1812, Lovie, now thirteen years old, and John, 20, have a son named Certus. (In a later census, his name is recorded as "Census.")

During the War of 1812, John Oden of North Carolina was in the military. He may or may not be our ancestor, who would have been a seaman. The John Oden name is found in many other North Carolina counties and all over the United States.

Someone posted their date of marriage as 1815. Lovie would have been sixteen. Did they have to wait until she was sixteen to marry?

In the 1830 census, John and Lovie have two children, one under nine years old. Either they lost that child or a child was visiting that day, because Charles Lamb was not born until 1835, when his father is forty-four and his mother thirty-seven. His sister Charlotte is born in 1837 and Sallie in 1838.

How do we account for the twenty-three years between the birth of Certus in 1812 and Charles Lamb in 1835? An old Bible somewhere may have records of additional births, still births or miscarriages, between Certus and Charles Lamb. I found Certus in early census, but not later. He may have left Hatteras as a young man. (I discovered a reference in Beaufort County to a will for a Certus Oden that mentions Sallie Ann Fulcher.)

In 1860, John tells the census taker that Rhode Island was his place of birth. John is listed with Lovie and daughters Charlotte and Sallie. In earlier censuses he had given Virginia and West Virginia as places of his birth. (West Virginia was not formed until 1861.)

Perhaps he thought he had been born in Virginia and only learned later that his place of birth was Rhode Island, on Christmas Day, 1792. Birth certificates were not initiated until 1913. When he died in 1873, the informant for his death certificate gave Virginia as his place of birth.

Judiah Oden, said to be John's father, was born in 1767 in colonial Virginia. John's mother, Charlotte, may have been from Rhode Island. Without a surname, I could not look for her there. (DNA may reveal the truth in years ahead.)

Lovie Alice Stowe's family

William Springer Stowe 1770-1855 and Millie Midgett 1770- 1850, the parents of Lovie Alice, were born in Currituck County and died in Hyde County. They never moved; were always residents of Hatteras Banks, but county designations changed for one reason or another.

Until 1846, Hatteras Banks was part of that 200-mile stretch from the Virginia line to Ocracoke Inlet and was in Currituck County. During Colonial times, Hatteras Banks was in Carteret County, part of the Colonial Carolinas.

In 1870 the North Carolina Legislature passed an act to form Dare County, named for Virginia Dare of Roanoke Island, the first English child to be born in America. Dare County was formed from sections of land formerly part of Tyrrell, Hyde, and Currituck counties in 1870.

Charles Lamb Oden and Sallie Ann Fulcher

Charles Lamb Oden and Sallie Ann Fulcher Oden

Charles Lamb,1835-1925 and Sallie Ann Fulcher, 1838-1921, were married November 29, 1855, by Joshua H. Daily in Hyde County, Frisco, North Carolina. In one census, Charles claimed they had had eleven children. The nine who lived to maturity and became heads of Hatteras families were:

Singleton Spires, 1858-1925; Andrew Peele, 1861-1937; Mogieannah,1862-1925; Lovie Alice,1868- 1896; Dexter S., 1870-1939; Victoria Dixon, 1873-1949; Laura C., 1876-1945; Moses Ransom, 1879-1948. A son, John C, , born in 1874 died in 1879. Reason of death is unknown.

Moses Ransom (Ranse), his wife Mathilda Gaskins, and their two daughters, Velma and Daisy, lived with his parents in the house in front of the graveyard, where all have graves, telling a sad story. Mathilda died in 1914 of tuberculosis. Both daughters died of the same disease, Daisy in 1921 and Velma in 1925.

Sallie Ann and Daisy's deaths in 1921, left Charles Lamb Oden, Ranse and Velma in the house. In 1925, Charles Lamb and Velma died, leaving Ranse alone. He was a widower for fourteen years when he became enamored of a young woman from Beaufort, North Carolina. Julia Sawyer, a teacher at the Hatteras school. They were married in 1928 in Beaufort.

ODEN GRAVEYARD

Early death records give Oden Graveyard as a burial place. Later the same cemetery is referred to as Oden-Austin Graveyard. The oldest daughter of Charles Lamb and Sallie Ann Oden, Mogieannah; her husband; their seven sons and their wives, and some of their children are buried there, but the cement dividers that once marked off seven Austin plots are now under sandy turf.

Another daughter, Lovie Alice, wife of Eugene Peele, died early and has a grave there. The other two, Laura and Victoria, are buried elsewhere.

When Moses Ransom died December 3, 1948, his will gives lifetime rights to the house to his wife Julia. Dementia eventually necessitated Julia be cared for somewhere off the island and before her death, the house fell into ruin. The direct descendants of Charles Lamb and Sallie Anne Oden and rightful heirs were in hundreds.

William Horton Austin, youngest son of Mogieannah, the last third-generation heir alive assumed responsibility for the property and had the two-story house demolished. He gave the property on which the house stood, along with the Oden-Austin graveyard to Hatteras for the formation of Hatteras Community Cemetery, a graveyard for all the descendants of John C. and Lovie Stowe Oden.

Oden and Austin families have shared life for generations on the island located approximately forty miles from mainland North Carolina. In one way or another, their families relied on the waters of the Pamlico Sound and the Atlantic Ocean for their livelihood.

All my life Sallie Ann Fulcher's vein carried Native American blood. Sallie Ann's father and grandfather, both named Jesse, married in London. Going back to 1583, there are five ancestors named Thomas Fulcher. Sallie Ann's mother was a Farrow. I have not been able to learn anything about the Farrows. Her ancestor, Capt. Thomas Fulcher, 1633-1691, was probably born in London. Her father, Jesse Fulcher, 1788-1841, was born in Portsmouth, Carteret County, North Carolina, in 1788 and died in Ocracoke, November 15, 1841, before Ocracoke and Hatteras became separate islands.

The unusual name Mogieannah may be our clue. Perhaps the mother of Sallie Ann, Delora Farrow, who married Jesse Fulcher, carried the gene that establishes our identity with original settlers of Hatteras Island.

Chapter 28

Early Ballance Generations

In 1656, a William Justice paid passage for William Ballance, believed to be the first Ballance to arrive in North Carolina from England. Capt. John Frame received 1,198 acres (about twice the area of Central Park in New York City) of land in what is now Charles City County, Virginia, April 26, 1656, for transporting twenty-four people, one of whom was William Ballance.

Thereafter, William Ballance enabled others to come by paying for their passage. His action was not entirely unselfish. His generosity enabled him to get more land by grants.

William Ballance first settled where the division line was made between Virginia and North Carolina. The line's correct location was in contention and those living in the area were charged taxes both in Virginia and North Carolina. (Reference: *The Ballance Family History,* p. 88, 99-100 -- William Ballance and Mary history and children, compiled by Ernestine Ballance Liverman; January 1982-1983, 929.273 B21 Vol 4 p. 88.)

According to history, the earliest first settlement was 1670. However, in 1663, John Harvey received a grant of 1,600 acres of land in Currituck. (Currituck is an Indian name that means "land of the wild goose.")

William Ballance III (1714-1733) was the first of ten children of William II and Mary Smith Ballance. His siblings were: Moses, 1715-1733; John, 1718-1789: Hezekian,1719; Ann, 1721; Bridget, 1723; Marey, 1727; Sarah, 1729; Elizabeth, 1732; and Elizabeth 1735.

William Benjamin Ballance, Sr., 1732-1795, son of John Ballance, migrated from the upper area of Currituck County to Hatteras Island to become a large landowner. His property was said to extend from Cape Hatteras to Ocracoke Inlet. His 1785 will divided property he had bought from Susanna Stowe between five of his children: William Benjamin, Jr.; Cornelius; Moses Ransom; Eliza; and Cortena.

In 1848, William B. Ballance, Jr. sold twenty-six and two-thirds acres of land to his sister Eliza's husband, George S. Rollinson.

Two hundred years later, my father tried to establish the lines of the original purchase from Susanna Stowe because William Dudley Austin, my father's great-grandfather, married Cortena Ballance. When Daddy discovered taxes were not being paid on a 13-acre tract of that land, contacted surviving heirs of George S. and Eliza Austin Rollinson and got deeds for the property they would have inherited had the property not been sold.

Thereafter, he paid yearly taxes on the property and began to search for the original lines of the Susannah Stowe property. He hired a lawyer, on contingency, to defend his claim. With the expectation of receiving a sixth share of the property on which my father was paying taxes, the lawyer continued his work beyond my father's death. My father died October 7, 1962.

Hatteras Banks had been part of Carteret County during Colonial America years. Currituck County, formed in 1668, then a precinct of Albemarle County, included Hatteras Banks. Hyde County next claimed Hatteras. Finally, when Dare County was formed from parts of three counties, Hatteras was included within its precincts.

When my father died in 1962, he left a piece of property as part of his estate that had an unclear title. Believing the property, divided and subdivided through the years, had once belonged to his forefathers, he bought each small parcel from living heirs. However, John S. Phipps of New York State, years before 1962, claimed it by reason of purchases.

Before his death, my father engaged a lawyer on contingency, for a sixth of the parcel of land, he parcel of land, consisting of something over thirteen acres.

Brother, Shanklin, died January 1979; his widow, Ruby Meekins Austin, became the defendant in his stead. My husband Donald E, Skakle, Sr, died, April 1980. At the time the litigation began in 1984, Ramona and Dr. Virgil A. Wilson had divorced after 26 years of marriage and she had married William Hunter in 1982. I had married Charles Fetterroll of Nanuet, New York, in 1983.

As the litigation continued, Sister Marjorie Austin Newton sold her portion to John Dell; Attorney McCowan sold his. The newest addition to Seagull Motel, owned by Carlos D. Oden and his wife, my sister Josephine sat on property the Phipps were claiming, as well. Perhaps the lawyer and Shanklin knew our ownership might be challenged again. The rest of us were ignorant of the possibility.

Before we asked and were allowed to defend as a group, I engaged Charles Beemer, my personal lawyers. His first month's charges came in the same mail as a check from Josephine, expressing her concern for me.

"I can't accept this!" I cried aloud. My impulse was to return her check.

Yes, I needed help. The lawsuit made it apparent my earlier retirement had been a mistake. I needed money, lots of it. I had taken a job with Blue Cross-Blue Shield and had become an l on-call pharmacist for Eckerds Drug Stores.

That afternoon, as I settled at the table at Blue Cross with several others, I uttered a prayer and I cried in my heart, "Lord, what shall I do?"

As clear as could be, I heard in my mind, "Trust Me!"

I knew it was God. I resolved to trust Him for the future, whatever that might be. In the months ahead as I cashed certificates of deposit and took savings to repay my sister and the lawyers, I often had doubts. Luckily, my former employer rehired me at the hospital and intervened on my behalf with the director of the hospital to have my salary be restored from my earlier employment.

Before I returned to Durham Country General Hospital and afterwards, when I was not scheduled there, I acted as a paralegal for our lawyer, Roy A. Archbell, traveling to Raleigh to the North Carolina Archives to peruse reels with old newspapers, tax records, census and evidence of the transfer of any acreage that might affect any part of the thirteen plus acres we were defending. I sought clues in the old colonial records for land grants as far back as 1711-12. Attorney Archbell accumulated over a thousand documents.

In the fall of 1987, the United States Court of Appeals for the Fourth Circuit in Raleigh heard our appeal. The judge decided the plaintiffs had waited too many years before challenging the earlier decision. With the stakes so high and a "big war chest" the plaintiffs did not yield. We felt we had a moral and emotional responsibility to continue the defense. The lawyers on both sides continued to wrangle.

At the end of 1989, our lawyer advised us to agree to a settlement. Neither party were able to prove unbroken title to the property. The proposed agreement would have the property developed by a partnership made up of plaintiffs and defendants.

Margie had sold and Shanklin's widow, Ruby, sold her lot to a local real estate company and their client. Josephine and husband Carlos paid the plaintiffs $50,000 to quit the suit. Only Ramona (Mona) and I remained in the fight.

On New Year's Day 1990, sister Mona and I drove to Dare County to sign the agreement to develop the property with our opponents. Our lawyer assured us that it should be completed within sixty days. However, the economy slumped; developers were wary. Time passed.

Mona and Bill Hunter were enjoying the cottage they had built. I no longer retained a lawyer. From time to time one of my sons would urge me to do something and I would begin to be anxious until I recalled that voice in my head: "Trust me!"

Mona reengaged our lawyer. I did not. I proposed to represent myself with God's help. Approaching sixty-five, I retired from the hospital in September 1990.

We could not reach agreement with the two managers of the proposed partnership. Weary of the whole, I wanted to be out of the partnership and release from the agreement to develop the property jointly. I wanted to prevent its burden to another generation.

One August afternoon in 1998, the two managers, Timothy Midgett and Terrell Smith, met Mone and me at Hunter Haven. I expressed my desire to be free of the obligations of partnership. Soon after that I was invited to a meeting in Raleigh.

Charles Fetterroll and I had divorced July 1990. I drove alone and found the building. Waiting for me in the boardroom of the imposing office building were the president of Bessemer Trust Company of New York, representing the Phipps interest, their two lawyers, and the two developers. The mahogany table in the carpeted, well-lit room was large and shiny.

They asked if I were willing to take another lot in trade for my interest, I replied that I was not averse to a like trade. "God is my attorney. We are all subject to His authority."

Some of them looked surprised. The bank president reassured me of their good intentions, but I was skeptical.

When next on Hatteras Island, I looked at the lot they had to offer and another in Buxton, ten miles north of Hatteras. I liked both and came home to Chapel Hill to think about it.

One afternoon as I was awaking from a nap, I heard in my mind, "Tell them what you want rather than taking what they want to give you." My Attorney had spoken.

Immediately, I went into my office, composed a letter requesting ocean front lot within the bounds of that I claimed. I did have emotional ties. In addition, I requested the Buxton lot. The combined acreage of the two lots was less than a third of my acreage. The developers were opposed to my having any part of the oceanfront.

Finally, in July 2000, I received notice of the transfer of both lots to me. Ramona would not be required to move Hunter Haven and would retain a lot across the street from Hunter Haven.

December 2001 my sons Andrew, Clifford and I formed Skakle Family Limited Liability Company and engaged a contractor to build Dare Dreamer on my ocean front lot at Hatteras. Eighteen years after my first attempt to build a house, it opened for its first rental, July 2002.

Chapter 29

The Earliest Austins of Hatteras Island

The genealogical organization "Family Search" identifies Thomas Austin, who married in Currituck about 1719, as the first Hatteras Austin. He was born in 1690, probably in England, He died in 1752.

In 1756, the second Thomas Austin (1735-1804) received a grant of 170 acres in Currituck County, Hatteras Banks; in 1760 he acquired an additional 144 acres. Thomas Austin and his four sons listed taxable property in the Currituck County, North Carolina, tax record of 1755. This Thomas Austin's four sons are: Thomas Jr.; William; Cornelius; and Daniel.

Three sons remained on Hatteras Island to raise their families. The fourth, Daniel (1763-1810), married Elizabeth Daniels, daughter of Joseph Daniels of Currituck, and was still listed there in the 1790 Currituck census. Daniel Austin was a soldier during the Revolutionary War, present at the skirmish at New Haven, Connecticut.

Thomas Austin (1770-1845) and Marina Zilphia Burrus (1755-1845) had two sons, William Dudley, Sr. (1794-1849) and Edmund (1813-1855), and a daughter, Elizabeth.

William Dudley Austin, Jr. (Willie) and Ann Olivia Midgett, his first wife, had three children: Courtney (1847-1945); Ellen Christine (1849-1917); and a son, who did not survive to maturity. The couple divorced and Ann remarried. Her daughter from the second marriage was Rebecca Gray, who married Edmund Daily O'Neal.

Willie married his uncle Edmund Austin's widow, Mathilda Eliza Styron April 2, 1859. Thus, the woman he called "Aunt Elizer" became his wife, according to the Hyde County registry. His cousins became his stepchildren.

(The children of Edmund and Mathilda Eliza Styron Austin were George W. Austin, Louisa Day, Valentine, William Moses, and Joseph F.)

Willie's oldest daughter Courtney married William Wise Gaskill, and their children grew up to have families responsible for a great deal of the growth and progress of Hatteras Village. Courtney lived past her 97th birthday. She is reported to have said: "I never left Hatteras Island and never wanted to!"

Her sister, Ellen Christine, married a man named Moses Foreman.

In the Federal Census of 1860, Willie listed himself as a mariner and head of a household of eighteen people. The mixed group included Willie's two daughters, Courtney and Ellen; Elizer's five children by Edmund Austin; and Willie and Elizer's infant sons: Harmon Dudley and William Wheeler. Besides their family, Margaret Burrus O'Neal, the widow of Urias O'Neal (who had died in 1848) and her children were with them.

Margaret O'Neal and Willie were first cousins. Their mothers, Cortena and Barbara Ballance, were sisters.

Harmon Dudley was born in 1858, William Wheeler in 1860. William, then two months old, is listed wrongly in the 1860 census as "Wilson."

Daddy mentioned an Aunt Mozelle, born in 1862, who died at twelve years of age. Daddy had chuckled when he spoke of Aunt Mozelle. I thought Barzilla, the third wife of William Dudley might have been her mother. That night Daddy spoke to me in a dream: "No, they decided Barzilla had enough children."

The next day, from a census that listed Willie and Barzilla together, I learned that Barzilla had birthed thirteen children, six of whom lived. Mozelle was own sister to Wheeler.

When William Dudley Austin, Jr. served the Union during the Civil War there were two forts on the island. *The Long Roll, Impressions of a Civil War Soldier*, was written by a Swedish-born young man, Private Charles Johnson from Minnesota. He kept a journal and made sketches while deployed on Hatteras Island, which give some idea of life on the island at the time.

Chapter 30

William Wheeler Austin and Mogieannah Oden

As village children, they shared customs, events, and experiences. Mogieannah was the first daughter of young parents. Wheeler was the second son of older parents, both married previously with other children.

Wedding photograph of Wheeler and Mogieannah

The photo of Mogieannah with William Wheeler shows a small woman with a slender nose and dark eyes. She was the third born of the nine children of Sallie Ann Fulcher and Charles Lamb Oden. As part of an intergenerational family, she learned to care for a home and family from her mother, Sallie Ann and her Oden grandmother, Lovie Alice Stowe. Interaction with many personalities taught her wisdom.

When they married, July 17, 1887, Mogieannah was twenty-three years old and William Wheeler, twenty-seven. Their first son, James Monroe, was born September 8, 1887. Andrew Shanklin, their second son, arrived February 20, 1889; Frederick Barrett, 1891; Lovie Alice, 1893; Beatrice, 1895; Ernest Lee, Nacie, and Luther Lathan were born two years apart. William Horton, born in 1907, was their youngest.

My Father's Name

Dr. Andrew Shanklin was born in Ireland, August 20, 1827, and died December 23, 1869, in North Carolina. His burial place is at St. Paul's Episcopal Church, Beaufort, Carteret County North Carolina.

Someone else received the name before my father did. In 1851 Comfort Burrus and Caleb Stowe, the brother of Lovie Alice Oden, named a son Andrew Shanklin. Did Dr. Shanklin deliver their son? Where was Andrew Shanklin Stowe born?

The 1850 census places Dr. Shanklin and his wife, Orpha, in Mattamuskeet, Hyde County, North Carolina. We do not know if Dr. Shanklin ever functioned as a doctor at Hatteras.

Probably, Mogie and Wheeler named their second son, born in 1889, after Grandfather Charles Lamb's cousin, Austin Andrew Stowe.

More of the Family

Wheeler served for twenty-seven years in what first was known as United States Life Saving Service. Two of his brothers-in-laws, Claughton M. Gray, husband of Victoria Oden; and Eugene H. Peele, husband of Love Alice Oden, served with him. Mogieannah's cousin, Charlie Lamb

Austin, named for her father was also part of their crew. The other crew members were Millard F. Ballance, Oliver G. Styron, and David E. Willis. During his later years of service, his monthly salary was sixty-five dollars.

All seven sons and two daughters of Mogieannah and Wheeler grew up and raised their families at Hatteras. During World War II, Nacie and Horton lived and worked elsewhere, but returned to Hatteras to live out their lives.

Wheeler claimed the children of Ellsworth Balance, widower of his daughter Lovie Alice, and Eliva Rollinson as his own. When Lovie Alice died in 1925 of blood poisoning, she left four children: Thurman, Myrtis, Wheeler and two-year old Gamaliel. Wheeler had been part of a mixed family himself. So, when Ellsworth remarried, he understood and sympathized.

When I was a small girl, Grandpa Wheeler went to Elizabeth City for a trip and brought me a small, Japanese paper umbrella and a bottle of Hoyt's cologne. I wonder now if he gifted all his many grandchildren. I remember our wrapping Christmas gifts for our many cousins.

When his youngest son William Horton married Violet Gaskill of Wanchese, N.C., August 27,1931, Grandpa Wheeler, lived with them. Horton had the old house demolished in 1935 and had a new, one-story house built. The old kitchen part was moved to the corner of the backyard.

Daddy bought a station wagon in 1937, intending to take his family to California. Perhaps the depression prevented that trip. Instead, he took Grandpa Wheeler, Mama, Mona and me on a sightseeing trip to Natural Bridge, Virginia. Picture taken at the time, record our stop in Wanchese at the Daniels homestead. Daddy, Mama, Mona and me are standing next to the wagon, with Grandpa Wheeler visible inside. All were wearing hats. One at Virginia destination is of Grandpa Wheeler, Mona and me, with the Natural Bridge as background.

When I visited Grandpa Wheeler during his last illness, I asked, "How are you feeling?" He chuckled. With a twinkle in his eye from his bed he replied: "With my hands and feet!"

Grandpa Wheeler died in 1941.

In 2020, William Horton, Jr. who resides in Roxboro, North Carolina, sold the house and property that had been the homestead of Wheeler and Mogieannah, with regrets. He had promised his father he never would, but his father, Horton, had replied: "Never say never!"

Chapter 31

The Daniels Family of Roanoke Island

Celia Pugh (April 2, 1819-February 8, 1849) a daughter of Little John and Charlotte Pugh of Lake Landing, North Carolina, married Thomas Rollins Daniels (August 8, 1825-Febuarary 27, 1855) of Wanchese, N.C., in 1844.

Their first son is John Thomas (1846-1911). Their second, George Charles (1849-1938). Celia died Feb. 8, 1849, seven days after the birth of George Charles.

In the census of 1850, Sarah T. Rollins Daniels, sixty-six years of age, is listed as head of household that includes her son, Thomas Rollins, age twenty, and his sons, John Thomas, four years old and one year old George Charles.

Sarah Rollins Daniels, born in Lambeth, London, England March 3, 1799, was the widow of Thomas Daniels. (Sarah received forty dollars for a half-year pension from his having served as an infantryman during the Revolutionary War. His death was in 1818.) She is listed as head of household.

Thomas Rollins became a seaman to provide for his two sons and his mother. A few years later, he married Celia's younger sister, Elizabeth McDaniel Pugh. In 1855, he dies at thirty, and his mother raises his two sons.

During the Civil War, John Thomas volunteered for the Confederate infantry. George, too young for the regular army, decided to volunteer to be a Confederate drummer boy. He started to leave, got as far as the gate. He decided his grandmother needed him more than the army. Sarah Rollins died December 1, 1869.

George Charles Daniels

George Charles Daniels married Nancy Cudworth in 1867 when he was eighteen years of age old, and at nineteen he became a father. Their nine children were: Mary Lucetta, 1868–1958; Thomas Daniels, 1870-1870; Charlie, 1872-1876; George G., 1874-1893; Celia Arletta, 1876-1969; Janetta, 1878-1878; Ethelbert (Tucker), 1879-1953; Claud, 1881-1883; and Ethen Crawford, 1883-1946. Four lived to grow old.

George Charles Daniels, Dare County Representative to the North Carolina Assembly

Daughters Lucetta and Arletta were out of the home, raising families of their own, when Nancy became ill. Sometime during the period of Nancy's illness, George asked Margaret Johnson and her daughter, Elrado, to be part of his household to care for Nancy, the home, and three sons still living there. The sons were George G., Ethelbert (Tucker), and Crawford.

Nancy Cudworth Daniels died May 5, 1886, and Margaret and Elrado stayed on to help George.

Chapter 32

George Charles and Margaret Ann Johnson's family

The Daniels Family on The Lane in Wanchese, North Carolina, and Night, the horse.

George and Margaret's children were Inez Lynn, 1890-1969; Lillian, 1892-1985; George Columbus, 1894-1977; Geter Pritchard, 1896-1897; Caswell Hobson, 1898-1980; Sarah Montez, 1901-1901; Thomas

Elden, 1902-1932; and Clarence Luther, 1904-1986. Elrado was eleven when my mother was born.

Mama, three years old at the time, recalled seeing the dead body of George G., an unmarried 19-year-old, on leave from the U. S. Lifesaving Service, of what they believed to be sunstroke. He died on the on the front porch of the homestead.

Margaret died in 1915 at age fifty-three. George lived to be eighty-nine and continued to work on the land until 1938, when a stroke took away his speech. No one knew what he was trying to say when he held up three fingers. Mama wondered if he was thinking of his three sons, Caswell, George, and Luther, who lived away from Roanoke Island.

He died August 24, 1938. His funeral service was at Bethany Methodist Church in Wanchese, where he faithfully attended worship and was often asked to pray.

Once a young man asked, "Mr. George, how do you know when to pray? You slept through the whole church service."

He replied, "Young man, I was not asleep. I was resting my eyes."

Hard of hearing, it is surprising he heard the pastor's request that he pray the closing prayer. He may have been resting his red, watery eyes. He suffered from something called "granulated eyelids."

Chapter 33

Stories by Inez Lynn Daniels Austin

I drove a horse and buggy. Old Dory was our mare. We paddled in the cutting sedge in shad boxes corked with hair or any old pieces of clothing, or cotton -- someone's share of the fixings for our dream boat that would take us in imagination anywhere. Down the canal to the Green Place or through the old Greater Gut -- to visit Uncle Sal and Aunt Ide and their old black, friendly mutt.

By footpath around the Club House run by Uncle Spence, we stop and visit Aunt Lovie, not far from the goose pen fence. She always had a cookie or a cool drink of water from a barrel. That was on a walk on the cool side of the house with a gourd or a conch in the gutter from which we drank our fill of the water from the rain barrel, never thinking of germs that many mouths may have left there, where our lips too had touched. Perhaps we were protected by nature's laws or such powers as helped eager, thirsty children as they munched their cookies.

It was time to be at home and a long way around, so we tied up our vessel and scooted around the Club House. But saw on the ground pieces of broken dishes. We could not leave them behind. With aprons lifted to form a sort of bag, we gathered the shining treasures, all our strength could wag.

A footpath through the cotton patch -- Bolls higher than our heads. We saw a Canadian goose sitting on her nest. She must have given a danger signal that a pest molested her. Her mate was on the scene quicker than we could think, honking in angry protest.

Quickly, through friendly cotton rows, we cautiously slinked until Mr. Gander no longer pursued us. Around the curves or rises of the ground we ran to get away to safety and search for other grand adventures unknown to any man, our broken crockery forgotten, for we had tossed it, as we ran, pursued by Mr. Gander."

GRANNY

I remember one little old lady who, in my childish way of thinking, was a tower of strength -- beauty. And why, I ask myself, did I have this feeling about the little old lady whose hump on her back, from what she explained to me, was white swelling when she was a girl. I believed her, of course, but I still wondered what caused the hump on her left shoulder.

She walked with a sort of quick step that made one feel she was easing her hurt shoulder. I do not know if this was so, though. Why would a child be attracted to an unbeautiful being? I think I have long ago given myself an answer: The little old lady with all that was not right with her physical self was overbalanced by the many virtues that she possessed as her natural heritage.

No one made finer molasses cakes, potato pies and other delicacies than this little old lady. She shared with others the fruits of her labors. If there was a child in her neighborhood that was feverish or ailing in any way, the little old lady with the hump and the quick step was mighty sure to be on hand to remember the sick child. How she learned about everything going on around her -- there were no telephones -- it must have been by "grapevine" communication.

She was an obstetric nurse, as we call them now. Then they were plain "Granny."

I could always tell when there was to be an addition in my neighborhood. Children even then were wiser than their elders gave them credit for being, although coming births were certainly not discussed among mother and children.

Granny was around frequently, helping with the quilting, the hog killing, pea picking and potato digging. By these signs I knew there was to be a new baby around soon.

A smart child could learn a lot by playing dumb and taking her dolls and sewing under the quilt when the ladies were quilting. They never realized that a little girl with her dolls was under the quilt for the express purpose of listening in, and when the talk above the quilt was interesting the little play mother beneath the quilt let her humming get exceptionally low and quiet so she could listen in better.

You see, it looked like the dolls were almost asleep and the humming was quieter so as not to awaken dolly. When in reality, "small pitcher" was exercising big ears. I never knew why the saying: "Small pitchers have big ears," but I put it that it meant a small child could listen in when she was supposed to be otherwise engaged.

Granny always had a wealth of knowledge to impart. That may have been one reason, along with food sharing, which endeared her to children and elders alike. She knew all about flowers and had a little flower garden in the right-hand corner of her rather large yard that was filled with flowers. Her white snowball tree -- hers was not a bush -- was in the right-hand corner of her flower garden. The fence was covered with honeysuckle, ivy, wisteria, and trailing rose bushes.

On the left of the garden walk was a velvet rose bush. The delight of delights came to me when for pulling weeds or helping to clear leaves from the garden, I was given a bunch of flowers from Granny's garden to take home. Her sweet shrub bush, I can still smell -- it was not a pretty plant. Just a little brown bud like an opening chestnut, but the perfume was as delightful as the sweet shrub perfume.

Her perfume was old Hoyt's German Cologne. She was never without it. She put a little on her white hair with Vaseline to keep her hair smelling sweet.

When Granny's sons or her "old man," she called her husband, was away from home, any child in the community considered it a treat to stay nights to keep Granny company. When bedtime was near, the coffee pot and milk pitcher were brought into the living room -- this on cold winter evenings. Cake or pie was brought in. There was this treat each night before we retired. I slept close to the hump on Granny's back.

She wore long night gowns. They were pretty to me. The yoke was tucks and insertions. A ruffle on neck and hand of over embroidery and the gown was starched and ironed. There must have been a drop or two of her cologne in the starch, for her nightie had that sweet shrub smell.

Then was then, now is the time to think of all the world as a peaceful, happy place, half buried in a feather bed, cold feet stuck close to a warm old lady's knees or there about, with her back turned toward the little sleeper. Oh no! She would never sleep face to you. She did not know a thing about germs, but she did not like children to get her breath. Perhaps she thought they would breathe too hard and take some power away from her. She was not a snuff-dipper, or one would think she had bad breath. She had dental plates, so there were no bad teeth to worry about. Perhaps her hump was better taken care of if she slept on her right side, because it was on her left shoulder.

Hog Killing Day

If on a Saturday morning, one might have for breakfast a link of home-made sausage, an egg, hot biscuits, home-made butter, jelly, and a glass of milk -- all home produced. People in those days, not all of them "good old days" as some people say, they were not too much concerned about the cost of living. They usually had to buy sugar, coffee, flour and sometimes meal. The rest of the food stuff was raised, but it took a lot of hard labor to produce food for a family. All the family helped.

Another Story of Helping-

At hog-killing time the children and the neighbors helped. The big iron pot, large enough to hold twenty buckets of water, had to be cleaned, put in a calm place on four bricks to heat water. It took a lot of water to clean and scald hogs and intestines, after they had been taken from the dead hogs, and to scald the dead hogs.

The children had to keep wood and chips in hand to keep the fire going. The haslet, it was called: liver, lights, heart, and the like, were soon prepared and placed on the number eight wood stove in the kitchen.

It took a lot of food to feed the women, men and children helping at a hog killing. The rutabagas, white potatoes, and sweet potatoes (baked) were prepared, ready to help with the menu. Dumplings of meal were added when the haslet stew was fifteen or twenty minutes from being tenderized sufficiently to add the bread. There were hot biscuits, also. It took a lot of feeding in the house by the side of the road at hog-killing time.

The hogs were washed and washed. Plenty of cold water from the well was thrown on the porker to cool it for cutting up to smoke or salt. Besides being warm already, the hogs had been soused up and down in a barrel of boiling water first, head down. Then back end up and down in the scalding water.

Two people carried the scalded hogs to boards laid out under the apple trees for the scraping job. Lots of kids could help at this job. I suppose the older folks had to complete the scraping job to get the hair and dirt off or was its dirt?

Perhaps it was the outer skin. Anyway, it scraped off down to white skin that only needed plenty of cold water to finish the animal off for the cutting boards. Usually this was done after night and that animal heat was sure to be out of the hog or the meat would get "pickle heated." That is when the skin softens and slips off to the touch when a big round of meat was pulled from the board in which it reposed.

The second night was lard cutting time. All the intestine fat and belly flab, it was called, was cut to be tried up in the big black pot the next day. After the lard was tried, it was packed in fifty-pound lard cans for future use, of course. The cracklings (left from the trying) were mashed fine and packed in stone jars to be used in corn bread and potato bread.

The third night -- sometime the fourth -- was sausage night. We borrowed a grinder and a stuffer from Aunt Ella Bailey, a neighbor. She usually got a ham or a shoulder for the kindness. The larger girls helped at the sausage making. Small children were not allowed in the kitchen around the knives or the cutters and grinder machines.

The stuffer was a machine without power. It had a half gallon round container, a handle to push down the meat into the casing. We used plain old gut from the hogs. We made some large bags, about four inches around, but it was not as good as the smaller round ones that were smoked, hung in the smoke house and later under the old white apple trees on rods. There was so much sage and red pepper in the meat and smoke on the casing that flies stayed away.

The spout was inserted into the casings. One person held the gut or casing in place. A second person fed the meat into a kind of hopper container. A third person manipulated the handle. You pushed it up and pulled it down. "Slowly there," you would hear to keep the gut from slipping off.

Most of the hog killing is by this time well taken care of, except the jowls and hogs heads, which are taken out of salt and put in the smoke house to be smoked along with the hams, shoulders, and sausage.

The fourth night the feet must be date-nailed (toenails had to be removed) over hot coals in the hearth of the cook stove. They must be scraped, singed, and cleaned. They are then boiled along with the skins off the belly fat and perhaps a hog head or two.

The tender boiled concoction now goes to the three-foot-long bread tray where it is worked over, de-boned and mixed with salt, pepper, and sage. When all this is complete, the souse is pressed down into pans or bowls under weights for two or three days, the hogs-head cheese is ready for the table.

We called it souse. That is the way it sounded and I like that name better. We did not souse many hog heads (as I said before). We just soused in the tray, after boiling tender, all the leftovers.

(Research revealed that souse is traditionally made from a whole boiled hog's head, but it can come from pigs' ears, knuckles, and feet (aka trotters), which yield enough natural gelatin to hold the mass together.)

Everything was used except the squeals. Hair, toenails, and intestine loads. We even vied with each other about who should get which bladder from which hog. We usually had the one from the hog we chose to call our own. Do you know what we did with the bladders? We cleaned them, blew them up like a balloon, put a dozen or so buck shot in them and hung them up to dry. We used the finished products as rattlers. We had not learned much about Halloween or they would have been nice noise makers for that occasion.

Corn Parching

Corn Parching was a fun thing with reward. The children always enjoyed a corn parching. They were sent to the corn crib and cautioned to bring red corn, as it was sweeter. I cannot see if red was sweeter than white, but I do know that red corn was a lot less plentiful than white. So, I decided the red-corn hunt got a lot of white ears shucked for the next day's feedings. (For the hogs)

Finally, when six or eight ears of red corn were found, shucked and de-silked, we were ready to shell the corn -- no easy job to be sure, but what cared we?

The pans were arranged on the dresser, the shelled corn put in them and pushed into the oven of the old #8. Raleigh was the stove's name. I still remember the bust of Sir Walter Raleigh standing out in bold relief on our oven door. They were kept bright and shining for many years, but after a long, long time, when the rest of the stove was getting worn, Sir Walter's bust began to show signs of wear too. The shine was no long there.

Well now, I got caught up with Sir Walter and almost forgot the corn. You had to keep stirring or shaking the corn back and forth to make it brown all over evenly. Burnt corn does not even pass for particularly good snuff.

After the corn was brown, we used the old-fashioned coffee mill seamed to the side of the chimney box and each child had a time to turn the handle. Each one had to grind his own corn. We did not know about Corn Flakes in those days. I do not suppose anyone had thought that far ahead. But we were getting our corn with the sugar added and before the night's festivities were over, we added the milk or water. It takes a lot of liquid to go along with parched, ground corn with sugar added.

One night one of the boys who tried to make a pig of himself was sick and upchucked. But I did not sympathize with him too much. His father was always a helper for my dad at corn saving and fodder stripping time so the sons also helped. The one who got sick on the corn could get the ears off the stalk a little faster than I. And he was taller and could get the fodder off the stalk faster than I could. He was always just a stalk or two ahead of me at the end of each row. He did wait for us to begin at the same time at every row's beginning.

Each row, I would think, "Well, this time I'll beat Wellie if I have to break my neck."

I did not break my neck but I did strip my right thumb nail off, right down to the roots I was working so fast. I was through working in the fodder for that day and more days to follow. I suppose Wellie had to do his row and my row too, but that did not keep me from feeling sorry when too much ground corn made him sick. I did feel sorry for Auntie Sara who had the cleaning-up job to do. I suppose my stripped nail might have been considered a sort of "eye for and eye and tooth for a tooth" thing. He got corn-sick and I was thumb-sick. One thing though, he got over his sooner than I did, so perhaps I was the worse transgressor. Who knows?

Mama enjoyed accompanying her father beyond the homeplace.

It was my good fortune to take trips with George Charles, Senior (writer's father) to a picnic for Sunday school. He did not like to miss one, either at Mann's Harbor, Wanchese or Manteo, in the North End, on or near the hills. Sometimes I attended speeches at Manteo in the Court House. I remember one especially well. J.Y Joyner, Superintendent of Public Instruction, was the speaker.

George Charles never sat way back. He either wanted to be near the speaker, the better to hear every word that was spoken, or perhaps it was a habit he had acquired from church attendance where he always sat up front in the "Amen Corner." I never understood why a certain place was for Amen.

The men of mature years occupied the upper left-hand corner of the old church at Wanchese. They did say "Amen" occasionally if the discourse was pleasing to their understanding. Now the Amen is seldom given in the Methodist Church. We have just as good, perhaps better preaching now than in the yesteryears of which I reminisce. But styles or habits change in everything else from dress to houses, so why not in style of showing appreciation?

I can look back over the years and I seem to hear a lot of those old "Ameners" giving "Amazing Grace how sweet the sound..." all the power of their lungs. They did put in a lot of grace notes where they were not written in the music, but they really had rhythm and gusto, if they lacked time and strict adherence to the tempo. I often wondered why the ladies sat in the middle or on the right-hand side away from their men folks. It was a rare thing to see men and women go in church together.

****

Epilogue

Andrew Shanklin Austin probably never weighed more than 145 pounds, even though he loved Eagle Brand milk, straight from the can. His physical appearance belied his strength of mind and stubborn determination. Out of respect and confidence in his counsel, people came to him for information he had stored in his agile mind.

His research covered years and required him to travel many miles as he sought to unravel the mysteries surrounding the land divisions of Hatteras Village. His research resulted in an accumulation of genealogical information. The binder, compiled by attorney Roy Archbell, contains my father's research notes. They were used for the legal defense of the property my father claimed.

Daddy once expressed a wish that he could be a doctor. Even though he did not become a doctor, generations to follow connected him to medicine.

After her marriage to Virgil A. Wison in 1950, Ramona helped him graduate in the first class of the University of North Carolina Medical School. Two of their four sons are in medicine. Dr. Stephen Craig Wilson is a Raleigh veterinarian and Dr. Adam S. Wilson of Washington State is an ENT specialist.

I received my degree in pharmacy from the University of North Carolina in 1949. My son Stanley Andrew married a pharmacist, Debbie

Coltrain. Their son, Austin Cole, is an internist, and their daughter in her last year of medical school intends to become an emergency room doctor.

My youngest son Clifford's daughter, Danielle Vidic, is a nurse at Duke Hospital in Durham.

Award-winning journalist Dennis Fisher once wrote: "Perseverance is as much about a strong don't as it is about a strong will."

Andrew and Inez built a home and a business and grew in God's grace. As a child and a young adult. I never realize until his death that I relied on his strength and stability my whole life. Despite his physical appearance and an aggravating heart condition, Daddy, by force of personality, character, hard work and sacrifice achieve his successes.

God gave my father a strong will and Mama. Together they were indomitable and influenced generations and a community by their values, their expectations, their labor, and their witness.

Acknowledgments

Three years ago, my son Clifford Skakle said, "Mom, I wish you would write about Pappy." Years before I wrote about Daddy under the title, "My Father Was a Boat Builder." Written before Word Processors and computers simplified and complicated our lives, the pages are full of errors and edits. It was never published.

Thanks to Elizabeth Newton, my niece, for lending her experience of over thirty years as copy editor for *Norfolk Virginian Pilot* to "our story." Jeffry Oden's comment: "Aunt Sybil, when you're gone, we will no one left to tell us how it was," added purpose.

Thanks to a genealogy group at Carol Woods retirement community where I have lived since 2016 and my nephew, Michael Wilson, who added me to his Ancestry account, encouraging adventure of discovery of the people who belong to us.

Thanks to Son Cliff for challenging me.

These extraordinary people share ownership of this manuscript.

A letter from another Dare County writer, David Stick, writing to thank me for my first memoir, *Confessions of an Outer Banks Filly*, is included here. His comments about my father and the men who were part of the Gooseville Gun Club era add interest to my story. His comments about my book warrant its inclusion. Maybe!

David Stick
Post Office Box 180
Kitty Hawk, NC 27949
November 24, 2004

Dear Sybil,

Yesterday, while sorting through an accumulation of old correspondence and other paper items in my loft, I came across *Challenges on the Home Front* and *Confessions of an Outer Banks Filly*, together with your card dated May 28, 2004.

I remembered, then, what I had done the day your card and *Challenges on the Home Front* arrived. I sat down right away and read your chapter about Hatteras during World War Two, then I called Manteo Booksellers to see if they had it in stock, only to learn for the first time about *Confessions of an Outer Banks Filly*, which I ordered from them. But I held off writing to you, partly because I wanted to read your book first, and partly because you had marked through your Chapel Hill address.

With my 85th birthday coming up next month, and a mild case of glaucoma, I have been trying to limit my reading to occasional short stretches during the course of the day. However, yesterday was an exception, for once I started reading *Confessions of an Outer Banks Filly* I found it so interesting, and in many ways your family years at Hatteras so similar to my own, that I didn't put it down until I had finished. I hope sales have been good, and that you have made arrangements to keep it in print, for it has a very important place in the factual history of the Outer Banks, as compared with the numerous volumes of fiction and folklore that seem to dominate todays output of literary works dealing with the Outer Banks.

As a one-time editor I tend to make pencil notes as I read, and on the second page I came across references to two men who were directly responsible for my father deciding to move his family to Dare County in 1929. Had it not been for them I might still be living in New Jersey, where I was born.

The men were Van Campen Heilner (not Van Kampen Heilner) and Albert Lyons (of Allenhurst, N.J., not Detroit)

First, Albert Lyons: He and his wife, Bess, their daughter, Alberta, and son George, lived in Allenhurst, the village adjacent to Interlaken, where I was born. Dad and "Uncle Bert" Lyons were avid fishing buddies, and the closeness spread over to the two boys in the families. They had a big limousine and a chauffer, who would pick me up at my Interlaken home frequently so George and I could accompany him on his regular trips to the nearby farming areas where he bought fresh vegetables and fruit. Occasionally we stayed overnight in each others home, and I still remember sweet smelling oval bars of soap that "Aunt Bess" had in the bathroom, instead of the ivory bars my family and most other people used. In the mid 1920s Dad made a couple of trips to Hatteras with "Uncle Bert", fell in love with the Outer Banks, and began making plans to move here.

Van Campen Heilner was another Lyons and Stick fishing buddy, but Dad's relationship with Heilner was different. Albert Lyons was an inventor who had suddenly struck it rich with his invention of the automobile bumper. Van Campen Heilner had gained a nationwide reputation for his articles and books on hunting and fishing, and in 1920 Van Campen Heilner and Frank Stick teamed up to write a book titled *The Call of the Surf*, in which each wrote alternate chapters, and Frank Stick paintings were used as illustrations. When I was a reporter for *The Raleigh Times* --I think it was 1940, the year, incidentally, when I went to a dance in Chapel Hill and met and danced with your sister Jo -- I was given the added job, but minus any added pay, of writing a weekly fishing column, titled "Angling Angles". I knew very little about fishing, since I had not inherited my father's love for the sport, so I decided that I'd better go down to the library and check out the most definitive books I could find on different kinds of fishing. The only one I could locate on surf fishing was *The Call of the Surf*. And in my family library now I have a copy of Van Campen Heilner's *A Book on Duck Shooting*, inscribed "To Frank, who has taught me a lot about duck shooting, from his old pal., Van."

I don't remember hearing about Dr. Hand, but "Harry" Stellwagen was another of the Lyons-Heilner-Stick fishing buddies I got to know.

Your father was an amazing man, and I had the good fortune to meet him on occasion, but by then he and Frank Stick were on extreme opposite ends of the Cape Hatteras Seashore matter. I do remember when I was in my middle teens and we were staying with Curt and Minnie Gray at the Buxton Club, my Dad let me take the car so I could drive little Billy Gray all the way down to Hatteras Village just so he could see his first movie. By then it was a Saturday evening ritual for me and my best friend and Skyco neighbor Louis Midgett to ride into Manteo in the back of his uncle's pickup truck, so we could attend the moomin pictures at the original Pioneer Theatre. It was, as I think your father's was also, silent movies, with periodic breaks to change reels.

You mention a Maurice Burrus house. I assume this was the same Maurice "Dick" Burrus, the only Outer Banker to become a major league baseball player, and a good friend of mine after he and his wife moved back home. He became a member of the Dare County Board of Education at about the time I served on the Board of Commissioners, but I lost track of him after he moved to Camden County.

Enough! My apoligies for being six months late. And again, congratulations on your contributions to the meaningful literature of our coastal area.

Cordially,

David

Biographical Sketch –

Sybil Austin Skakle, 1949 graduate of the University of North Carolina, raised three sons and in 1967 began work as a hospital pharmacist, retiring in 1990. Since retirement she has published seven books: *Searchings- rocks revelations rainbows*, 2001 and *Loves and Lives of Living and* Loving, 2005, with limited copies, are poetry books. Her published memoirs are *Confessions of an Outer Banks Filly*,2002; *Valley of the Shadow*,2009; *What Came Next,* 2014. In 2017 she *wrote* for, compiled, edited and published *The Story of Amity United Methodist. Who Plays on Court One,* published in 2018, is a novel for young readers.

Made in the USA
Middletown, DE
10 September 2024

60725648R00096